I0435140

Butterfly Gardening Using Southern Native Plants

TINA SAMUELS

Butterfly Gardening Using Southern Native Plants

By Tina M. Samuels

Cover Photo: (C) Mark Dreiling of Santee, CA

(C) 2015, all rights reserved

No portion of this manuscript shall be used without express written permission of the author

Table of Contents

Preface

Mark Dreiling was the photographer of all butterfly photos used and I thank him kindly for his allowing me the pleasure of their beauty.

Plant photographers were either from Larry Allain's permission or in public domain use from the Plants Database. I appreciate Mr. Allain's allowing me to use his photographs.

Each butterfly's description is repeated as needed throughout the book. This is done for easier reference. Each butterfly's info was researched off the Dallas Butterflies website and the Butterflies and Moths of North America website.

When referencing the NatureServe Global Status Rating, it is a non-profit organization that ranks the rarity of butterflies and moths at a global level. There are six rankings; GU – unranked, G1 – critically imperiled, G2 – imperiled, G3 – vulnerable, G4 – apparently secure, and G5 – secure.

Chapter One: Butterfly Gardening

Monarch Male
(C) Mark Dreiling of Santee, CA

No matter where you live in the United States, with a bit of preparation you can enjoy the beauty and grace of butterflies in your own butterfly garden. Once you understand a few basic principles, your garden will come alive with the flight of these beautiful creatures. The natural habitat of butterflies is constantly being destroyed as land is bulldozed for more buildings. Any effort on your part will be an aid in the conservation of the gentle winged wonders.

Where to Have Your Garden

While it would be wonderful to have the space to plant a large garden, with a wide variety of flowers and plants, set in an idyllic location, it is not necessary. You may use a window box, or an empty barrel to create a place for butterflies to come to. The important consideration in the placement of your garden is the sun. Butterflies prefer to be out in the full sunlight. Find the sunniest part of the yard, or the window that gets the most sun, and start your planning there.

Butterfly Research

A quick trip to the library, or search online, will tell you what types of butterflies are indigenous to your area. Once you know the butterfly types, you can find out which plants or flowers to use to attract them. It does you no good to have flowers that attract butterflies that live on the other side of the country.

What to Plant

To attract and keep butterflies in your garden you will need two different types of plants.

• Nectar plants are used to attract the butterflies. These plants are colorful. Plant a few varieties of these since butterflies prefer to have a choice in what they eat. It is best if you plant the different flowers in groups instead of having single flowers alternating in your design making them easier to be found. You may want to arrange them by size, building around the tallest flowers, so the smaller ones can be easily seen.

• Host plants are where butterflies lay their eggs. While host plants may flower, they are usually green, leafy plants. Once hatched, the larvae and caterpillars will eat these plants. Fit host plants between the groupings of nectar plants to allow the small butterflies to be able to reach the nectar plants without having to travel far. It will also help to hide the well-eaten leaves of the host plants as the larvae grow. However, if you have the host plants where they can be seen, you will be able to watch the butterfly emerge from its chrysalis. A sight sure to delight everyone in the family.

In a large garden, planting both types of plants is not a problem. Smaller, window box gardens may take a bit of arranging to achieve a look you are happy with. Having both nectar and host plants will keep the adult butterflies around longer, and keep a new supply of young ones coming for the whole season. Talk to the people at the garden center. While it is possible to buy and plant flowers that are not naturally native to your area, it is best to have plants that will thrive in your locale. The less time you have to spend picking out dead or withering plants, the more the butterflies will come around. Remember, host plants will be chewed, this does not mean you need to cull them out. They may not look great, so you may want to keep them behind the nectar plants, just not too far away.

When to Plant

Try having flowers that will bloom at different times of the season, and open at different times of the day. This may mean you are planting your flowers a few weeks or even a month apart. You could plant five or six seeds in an area, and then a week or two later plant another five or six in the same area to keep them blooming for a longer period. If you are using seedlings or plants, you could do the same thing, staggering the plantings. The idea is to keep as much color for as long as possible.

Many annuals will bloom from spring all the way through to fall, but will need to be replanted every year. They will provide vibrant color throughout the season. Perennials, on the other hand, will last from year to year, but will need to be cut back regularly or they will take over the garden. They offer more variety to their color than annuals. It is a good idea to have a mixture of both if you have the space. Remember to remove any dead blooms to keep new ones coming.

The height of butterfly season is late summer to early fall. This is when you will want to have your flowers in full bloom. Having some that are blooming earlier will start the trail to your garden, allowing them to lay their eggs to hatch for the summer. Keeping some flowering into the fall will give the last stragglers a place to lay their eggs, going dormant until the next year.

Where to Plant

Butterflies love to bask in the warm sunshine. If possible, have the majority of your garden in the sunniest spot of your yard. They will need a place to go if it rains, or gets too hot though. A nice, broadleaf bush will do; plant one off to the side of your garden. If you are in an apartment, use the sunny spot of your patio or balcony. If there is a tree or bush off to the side, even better. If you have no place for shelter, you can always put up a butterfly house to protect them during inclement weather.

Decorations

Some type of water supply would round out the necessities for butterflies. They like to congregate at puddles, especially the males. In a large garden, this could be a birdbath. If you are working in a small, container garden, a small bowl embedded in the dirt will do. A small, trickling fountain would add a pleasant sound to the sights and scents of the garden while giving them a watering hole. You could also hang a butterfly feeder if you want to have more nectar available to them than room allows. It also makes a nice decoration in a large garden.

Pesticides

The use of commercial pesticides will kill your butterflies. While it may be hard to remember, butterflies are insects, not small birds. The larva cannot eat leaves that have been sprayed with insecticides, so they will never make it through their metamorphosis to butterfly. If you have other insects that are eating your plants, plant smelly flowers like marigolds to keep them away. If you absolutely must spray against insects, use a gentle soap to wash them away instead.

No matter the size of your butterfly garden, you will want to have a seat or two nearby to enjoy it. This may become your relaxing place. A stone bench, an iron bistro set, or even a cozy window seat would be a wonderful place to sit and watch the butterflies flitting by and smell the sweet aromas of your garden.

Chapter Two: Native Gardening

The most beautiful, breathtaking gardens in the world are not really gardens at all, but nature. When it comes time to do your landscaping, take a hike and look at all the wonder around you, then use what you see to create your garden. Using plants and flowers that are native to your area will give create a space that requires little maintenance to keep its beauty.

Why Use Native Plants

Having a garden designed with plants and flowers that are native to your area has many advantages, and is quite beautiful. Since the plants are adapted to your climate, they will grow and thrive with little care from you. You will not need to worry about mulching to keep roots warm, or covering them from the harsh heat in the summer. They will grow perfectly well, probably even better, without your interference.

Native plants are more resistant to disease than non-native plants. They have grown in the area for years, developing immunities to any natural diseases of the area. Non-native plants are not only susceptible to any problems native plants have already overcome, they also have the risk of harboring new diseases to give to already established native plants. Trying to adjust the soil and water to accommodate both native and non-native plants can be tricky too. Some plants need to have a more porous soil than others do. The need for clay or moss to keep the plants healthy would mean adjusting the soil contents. Some plants require a higher pH in the soil than others do, now you have to consider adding ash or bone to the soil.

To mix native and non-native plants in your yard, you would need to have two separate gardens. The native garden would thrive on its own while you tended to the non-native garden.

Getting Started

Once you have taken a hike, or at least gone to a few local parks, go to the local garden center and talk to the people who work there. They will show you the different plants and flowers that are native to the area. The vast number of what is available will surprise and delight you. Even dessert areas have a huge variety of plants available to them.

Preparing the Ground

Now that you have a good idea of what you can plant, take a good look at the ground you will be planting in. Unless the topsoil has been removed, there will be no reason to add anything when you are planting native plants. They are accustomed to the nutrients in your soil, adding anything would be a detriment to their growth. If the area has been planted for a few years, you may want to add a natural fertilizer to replace diminished nutrients once the plants start growing.

It is up to you whether to get rid of any grass growing where you will be planting. If you are planting wild flowers, you merely need to trim the grass and scatter the seeds. If you want a defined garden, it may be best to kill off any weeds or grass growing there now. It is best to till up the ground first, but only one to two inches to avoid any deep seed from germinating.

Designing the Garden

You do not need to have every inch of land covered with flowers. Consider other bits of nature in your garden. A large rock outcropping, or a fallen log, adds to the natural beauty of the space. Have groupings of flowering plants with green leafy plants mixed in. Be sure to keep shorter flowers and plants in front of taller ones to keep them from getting lost. Consider adding in a small pool or pond for an added pleasure. If there is an electric supply nearby you can have a small fountain or waterfall. Planning and designing a native garden is the hard part, you want it to last for many years, keeping its beauty. There is no need to have it all done at the beginning of the season. You may want to consider taking a few years to get it just right; adding in plants as you get the feel of it all. No matter where you live, you will be able to pick and choose all kinds of sizes, colors and textures for your garden. Choose some plants that will come back year after year with no replanting needed –perennials; or choose some of the unique, vibrant annuals you will need to mow down and replace next year. A good mixture of both makes your garden a sight to behold.

Planting

Once you have picked the spot for your garden, and picked the flowers, you need to get them planted as soon as possible. You do not want to have them sitting out in pots for a day or two, waiting to be planted, be sure to keep them in the shade while you are working with other plants.

To create a garden that looks natural, do not plant your flowers in neat rows. Think of how they grow naturally. Plant groups of the same flower together, in small bunches. Leave open spaces between groupings or fill the spots in with ground cover.

Wildlife

One of the distinct advantages to having a native garden is the wildlife. Do not be surprised to see birds, butterflies, and small animals in your garden. This is all part of nature. You do not want to have so many visitors they completely destroy your garden, but they can be useful in keeping overgrowing perennials or ground cover from taking over the place. They are also useful for natural fertilizer. Birds will help keep insects away, with other animals chasing off the birds. With time, it will become its own ecosystem.

Maintaining Your Garden

A garden comprised of plants native to your area will need to be maintained, but not nearly as much as one containing non-native plants. There will be yearly pruning of trees and bushes, replanting of annuals, and deadheading blooms to keep more blooms growing. You may want to have plants that keep away bugs planted to avoid having to use an insecticide if birds are not doing the trick. Otherwise, letting the garden take its own course may be the best thing for it.

While there will always be some plant or flower that you absolutely love that is not native to your area, it is best to keep them to a small, regulated spot in your yard. They may thrive and be gorgeous, they may survive but not truly bloom and thrive, or they may not make it at all. To have a beautiful garden, it is best to have plants that will grow, thrive and bloom, turning your yard into a natural wonder.

Chapter Three: Wildflowers, Flowering Plants, and Vines

By choosing to incorporate native annuals and perennials in your garden habitat, you are not only encouraging native diversity; you are offering food to native butterflies. In many areas, native plants are facing near extinction, along with the wildlife that depends on the plants for sustenance.

Some butterflies are found in a small area, feed on a certain type of flower's nectar, or may lay their eggs on only one type of plant. For instance - the larvae of Monarch butterflies only eat from the milkweed plant. Many consider this plant a weed, but it is an important part of the Monarch's continued existence.

Native plants are an important part of your garden's eco-system. While imported seeds and plants may grow well, some are invasive and will choke out the native plants so sorely needed by local butterflies. One example on the extreme end of this is the kudzu plant. Originally brought to America as a cheap, fast growing food source for farm animals, kudzu is known as the 'Plant That Ate the South'. This plant has killed entire forest ranges due to its ability to grow faster than native plants and trees. It strangles them by growing around them, starves by absorbing sunlight and nutrients in the soil, and dehydrates by drinking all of the groundwater available.

When planning your butterfly garden, look first at local nurseries that cater to the needs of your area. You may be able to find native annuals and perennials low cost. You may also check with local farmers or other gardeners and offer to take away their 'weeds', most of which are native plants in need of a loving home.

Black Cohosh (*Actaea racemosa var. racemosa*)

Also Known As: Black Bugbane, Black Snakeroot, Bugbane, Fairy Candles, *Cimicifuga racemosa*

Plant Description: Growing 3 to 6 feet tall, this bushy plant has compound leaves and fuzzy flowers. Leaves are toothed while flowers are tiny and white and look like candles. Blooms should appear between May and August. Fruits are tan and berry-like.

Growing Guide: To grow a black cohosh, plant it in partial shade to full shade with a moist acidic soil. It does especially well with an hour or two of morning sunlight. Propagate by root division or by seed. Divide the plant in fall or spring or plant seed in the fall.

Interesting Facts: This was a snakebite remedy back in the 1800's. The root was used for that and for inflammation of the lungs.

Warnings: It does not have a pleasant odor.

Southern Distribution: Alabama, Arkansas, Georgia, Mississippi, North Carolina, South Carolina, Kentucky, Virginia, Tennessee, and West Virginia.

Classification: Family *Ranunculaceae* – Buttercup family

Genus *Actaea* L. – baneberry

Species *Actaea racemosa* L. – black baneberry

Variety *Actaea racemosa* L. *var. racemosa* – black cohosh

Butterflies and Moths Attracted: It is a larval host to the Spring Azure (*Celastrina ladon*). The spring azure has an apparent secure rating on NatureServe Global Status with a G4 rating. Its wingspan is between 7/8-inch and 1 3/8-inches. It has an upperside of a blue forewing and a gray-white underside.

Spring Azure
(C) Mark Dreiling of Santee, CA

Pearly-everlasting (*Anaphalis margaritacea*)

Also Known As: Western Pearly Everlasting

Plant Description: Growing 1 to 3 feet high in an erect form, this plant is often found clumped together. Leaves are narrow, gray-green or wool-white, and perennial. Flowers are white with a yellow center and on wooly stems. Bloom season is between June and October.

Growing Guide: The pearly-everlasting prefers full sun or partial shade with a dry soil. Propagate by division or seed. Seed should not be treated and sown in the fall. Divide in the spring, if you prefer that method.

Interesting Facts: This native has been used in dried flower arrangements and was once a folklore remedy for burns.

Southern Distribution: North Carolina, Tennessee, Virginia, and West Virginia.

Classification: Family *Asteraceae* – Aster family

Genus *Anaphalis* DC. – pearly everlasting

Species *Anaphalis margaritacea* (L.) Benth. –pearly everlasting

Butterflies and Moths Attracted: It is a larval host to the American Lady (*Vanessa virginiensis*) and the Painted Lady (*Vanessa cardui*) butterflies. The American lady has a NatureServe Global Status of G5, or secure, and a wingspan between 1 3/4-inches and 2 5/8-inches. There is brown, orange, and yellow in an uneven form on the upperside. A black patch and orange area with a white dot is on the forewing. There are two large eyespots on the hindwing's underside.

The painted lady is secure with a G5 NatureServe Global Status and has a wingspan between 2-inches and 2 7/8-inches. It has orange-brown wings with a darker base of the wings and an underside of black, brown, and gray. Undersides have four small eyespots. The forewing has a white edge bar and a black patch on apex. The hindwing has black spots in five rows and could have blue scales depending on butterfly.

American Lady
(C) Mark Dreiling of Santee, CA

Woman's Tobacco (*Antennaria plantaginifolia*)
Jennifer Anderson @ USDA-NRCS PLANTS Database

Woman's Tobacco (*Antennaria plantaginifolia*)

Also Known As: Everlasting, Plantain-leaf Pussytoes, Mouse Ear

Plant Description: Woman's tobacco grows up to one-foot high and one-and-a-half-feet wide. There are basal leaves that are evergreen and silver-green. Flowers are pink or white in a terminal cluster. Flowers are rayless and have a fuzzy appearance. Bloom season is between March and June.

Growing Guide: This native prefers to grow in full sun or partial shade and with a dry acidic soil. There is a high drought tolerance. Propagate by root division or by seed.

Interesting Facts: Flower heads look like a cat's paw and is the reason for its common name of 'pussytoes'.

Warnings: This is a winter deer browse and therefore will not have any deer resistance.

Southern Distribution: Alabama, Arkansas, Florida, Georgia, Kentucky, Lousiana, Mississippi, North Carolina, South Carolina, Tennessee, Virginia, and West Virginia.

Classification: Family *Asteraceae*– Aster family

Genus *Antennaria* Gaertn.– pussytoes

Species *Antennaria plantaginifolia* (L.) Richardson– woman's tobacco

Butterflies and Moths Attracted: It is a larval host to the American Lady (*Vanessa virginiensis*). The American lady has a NatureServe Global Status of G5, or secure, and a wingspan between 1 3/4-inches and 2 5/8-inches. There is brown, orange, and yellow in an uneven form on the upperside. A black patch and orange area with a white dot is on the forewing. There are two large eyespots on the hindwing's underside.

Groundnut (*Apios americana*)
Robert H. Mohlenbrock @ USDA-NRCS PLANTS Database / USDA SCS. 1989. Midwest wetland flora: Field office illustrated guide to plant species. Midwest National Technical Center, Lincoln.

Groundnut (*Apios americana*)

Also Known As: Wild Potato, Indian Potato

Plant Description: Growing 6 to 10 feet, this perennial vine has green leaves and red-brown or burgundy flowers. It blooms between July and September and then has seedpods that look like peas in fall.

Growing Guide: Grow a groundnut in wet or moist soil with shade. Propagate this plant by its seed. It will die back every winter and regrow.

Interesting Facts: The tubers and the seeds are edible and were relied upon by first Massachusetts' Pilgrims.

Warnings: This plant can take over a garden if you let it.

Southern Distribution: Alabama, Florida, Georgia, Kentucky, Louisiana, Mississippi, North Carolina, South Carolina, Tennessee, Texas, Virginia, and West Virginia

Classification: Family *Fabaceae* – Pea family

Genus *Apios* Fabr. – groundnut

Species *Apios americana* Medik. – groundnut

Butterflies and Moths Attracted: It is a larval host to the Silver-spotted Skipper (*Epargyreus clarus*). With a secure NatureServe Global Status rating of G5, the silver-spotted skipper butterfly isn't near extinction. It has a wingspan of 1 3/4-inches to 2 5/8-inches. There are forewing gold spots and a hindwing with a silver band on this black or brown-winged butterfly. The hindwing of a silver-spotted skipper will be lobed.

Silver-spotted Skipper
(C) Mark Dreiling of Santee, CA

Spreading Dogbane (*Apocynum androsaemifolium*)

Also Known As: Bitterroot, Flytrap Dogbane, *Apocynum androsaemifolium var.*

incanum

Plant Description: Growing two to five feet high, this perennial has oval leaves and bell-like pink flowers. Flowers are on the tips of the branches and bloom between June and August. They have a similar scent to the lilac plant.

Growing Guide: Spreading dogbane needs a dry sandy or gravelly soil and any type of lighting. Propagate by seed that have had two months of cold moist stratification.

Interesting Facts: This is a relative of the milkweed plants. The rolled stem fibers have been used to make twine, netting, bowstrings, and fabric.

Warnings: The sap is poisonous and can blister sensitive skin.

Southern Distribution: Alabama, Arkansas, Georgia, North Carolina, Tennessee, Texas, Virginia, West Virginia

Classification: Family *Apocynaceae* – Dogbane family

Genus *Apocynum* L. – dogbane

Species *Apocynum androsaemifolium* L. – spreading dogbane

Butterflies and Moths Attracted: It is a food source for the Monarch (*Danaus plexippus*) butterfly. The monarch has a G5, or secure, NatureServe Global Status and a large wingspan of 3 3/8-inches to 4 7/8-inches. Looking much like a viceroy, it has white spots on the apex and borders. Males are orange with black veins and borders and the females have orange-brown with black borders and blurry black veins. There are scent scales on the hindwing.

Indian Hemp (*Apocynum cannabinum*)
Larry Allain @ USDA-NRCS PLANTS Database

Indian Hemp (*Apocynum cannabinum*)

Also Known As: Dogbane, Hemp Dogbane, Prairie Dogbane

Plant Description: Growing 3 to 4 feet tall, this perennial has long leaves and small flowers. Stems are purple and erect. Leaves are green with whitish bloom on them. Flowers are clustered and cream in color. Seeds are in pods. Flowers will bloom between May and August.

Growing Guide: Plant this perennial in partial shade with a moist soil. It can work well in a variety of soil conditions.

Interesting Facts: There are many uses to Indian hemp. It has been used for cording. Its sap has been used as chewing gum. Medicinally, its berries were once used as a diuretic and as a heart tonic. Choctaw Native Americans chewed the root and swallowed its juice as a treatment for syphilis. It is said to induce sweating and vomiting when taken internally. Today, we are aware of its poisonous properties and would not be ingesting it.

Warnings: All parts to this plant are toxic due to cardiac glycosides and resins. Do not ingest. It is also weedy in some parts and can become invasive.

Southern Distribution: Alabama, Arkansas, Florida, Georgia, Kentucky, Louisiana, Mississippi, North Carolina, South Carolina, Tennessee, Texas, Virginia, and West Virginia.

Classification: Family *Apocynaceae* – Dogbane family

Genus *Apocynum* L. – dogbane

Species *Apocynum cannabinum* L. – Indian hemp

Butterflies and Moths Attracted: It is a food source for the Banded Hairstreak (*Satyrium calanus*) butterfly. The banded hairstreak has a NatureServe Global Status of G5, secure, and a wingspan of one-inch to 1 1/2-inches wide. There is a short and a long tail on the brown hindwing. Underside is darker with dark colored dashes with white edges. There is a blue tail spot and some orange near the tailspot.

Eastern Red Columbine (*Aquilegia canadensis*)
Jennifer Anderson @ USDA-NRCS PLANTS Database

Eastern Red Columbine (*Aquilegia canadensis*)

Also Known As: Wild Red Columbine

Plant Description: Growing up to 2 feet in height, this perennial has red or yellow nodding flowers and green or blue-green compound leaves. Foliage is semi-evergreen and blooms arrive between February and July. Fruits are tan capsules.

Growing Guide: For best results, plant an Eastern red columbine in partial to full shade and alkaline to nearly neutral pH soil. It is both cold and heat tolerant. Soils should be well drained and moist for best growth conditions. Propagate by seed, as division is often difficult. Seeds should have up to a month of cold moist stratification prior to sowing.

Interesting Facts: The seeds were crushed and rubbed onto the skin by Native Americans to attract women.

Warnings: Do not over water this plant as it can cause rot in the crowns. Also, do not plant in full sun areas as leaves could burn and the plant can become stunted.

Southern Distribution: Alabama, Arkansas, Florida, Georgia, Kentucky, Mississippi, North Carolina, South Carolina, Tennessee, Texas, Virginia, and West Virginia.

Classification: Family *Ranunculaceae* – Buttercup family

Genus *Aquilegia* L. – columbine

Species *Aquilegia canadensis* L. – red columbine

Butterflies and Moths Attracted: It is a larval host to the Columbine Duskywing (*Erynnis lucilius*) butterfly in the areas of Kentucky and Virginia. The Columbine duskywing is apparently secure with a G4 NatureServe Global Status and has a wingspan of 1 3/16-inches to 1 5/8-inches. It is dark brown with a brown patch by the forewing's end. The underside has rows of pale spots on the hindwing. Females have a scent scale patch while males have yellow scent scales on a costal fold.

Virginia Snakeroot (*Aristolochia serpentaria*)

Also Known As: Virginia Dutchmanspipe, *Aristolochia convolvulacea, Aristolochia hastata, Aristolochia nashii*

Plant Description: This perennial grows 8 to 24 inches tall with narrow heart-shaped leaves with purple-brown flowers. Bloom season is between May through July.

Growing Guide: Grow in full shade conditions with a dry well-drained soil. It should be propagated by seed.

Southern Distribution: Alabama, Arkansas, Florida, Georgia, Kentucky, Louisiana, Mississippi, North Carolina, South Carolina, Tennessee, Texas, Virginia, and West Virginia

Classification: Family *Aristolochiaceae* – Birthwort family

Genus *Aristolochia* L. – dutchman's pipe

Species *Aristolochia serpentaria* L. – Virginia snakeroot

Butterflies and Moths Attracted: It is a larval host to the Pipevine Swallowtail (*Battus philenor*) butterfly. This butterfly is secure, with a NatureServe Global Status of G5. Its wingspan is 2 3/4-inches to 5-inches, making it a moderate-sized butterfly. It is distinguished by its blue iridescent colored hindwing and its row of seven orange dots on the underside of its hindwing.

Pipevine Swallowtail
(C) Mark Dreiling of Santee, CA

Common Dutchmanspipe (*Aristolochia tomentosa*)

Also Known As: Woolly Dutchman's Pipe, *Isotrema tomentosa*

Plant Description: It grows 20 to 30 feet with large leaves and trumpet-like flowers. Foliage is deciduous and heart-shaped. Flowers are yellow-green in color and can be hidden by the leaves. Blooms can be anytime between March and May. Seeds are in ribbed capsules that are gray-brown when mature.

Growing Guide: This vine prefers full sun or partial shade and a rich moist well-drained soil. It will not tolerate a dry soil. Propagate by seed.

Interesting Facts: The common name comes from the flowers looking like a Dutch smoking pipe.

Southern Distribution: Alabama, Arkansas, Florida, Georgia, Kentucky, Louisiana, Mississippi, North Carolina, South Carolina, Tennessee, and Texas.

Classification: Family *Aristolochiaceae* – Birthwort family

Genus *Aristolochia* L. – dutchman's pipe

Species *Aristolochia tomentosa* Sims – common dutchmanspipe

Butterflies and Moths Attracted: It is a larval host to the Pipevine Swallowtail (*Battus philenor*). This butterfly is secure, with a NatureServe Global Status of G5. Its wingspan is 2 3/4-inches to 5-inches, making it a moderate-sized butterfly. It is distinguished by its blue iridescent colored hindwing and its row of seven orange dots on the underside of its hindwing.

Swamp Milkweed (*Asclepias incarnata*)
Jennifer Anderson @ USDA-NRCS PLANTS Database

Swamp Milkweed (*Asclepias incarnata*)

Also Known As: Pink Milkweed

Plant Description: Growing 2 to 4 feet tall, this milkweed has large terminal flowers that are deep pink or rose-purple in color. Leaves are opposite and lance-like in appearance. Seedpods are tan or brown and long. Expect flowering between June and October with the swamp milkweed.

Growing Guide: Swamp milkweed prefers sun or partial shade with a wet or moist soil. Soils should be nearly neutral in pH or lightly acidic. Propagate by seed or by division. If dividing the plant, it should be done in the spring.

Interesting Facts: While it is poisonous raw, many cook the plant and eat it. Buds of the flowers, leaves, seedpods, shoots, leaves and flowers can all be boiled and simmered for a food source.

Warnings: All parts of this milkweed have cardiac glycosides and resinoids that are toxic and can, upon ingesting raw, give the person symptoms of vomiting, spasms, weakness, and stupor.

Southern Distribution: Alabama, Arkansas, Florida, Georgia, Kentucky, North Carolina, South Carolina, Tennessee, Texas, Virginia, and West Virginia.

Classification: Family *Asclepiadaceae* – Milkweed family

Genus *Asclepias* L. – milkweed

Species *Asclepias incarnata* L. – swamp milkweed

Butterflies and Moths Attracted: It is a larval host the Monarch (*Danaus plexippus*) and Queen (*Danaus gilippus*) butterflies. The monarch has a G5, or secure, NatureServe Global Status and a large wingspan of 3 3/8-inches to 4 7/8-inches. Looking much like a viceroy, it has white spots on the apex and borders. Males are orange with black veins and borders and the females have orange-brown with black borders and blurry black veins. There are scent scales on the hindwing.

The Queen has a G5, or secure, NatureServe Global Status and a wingspan between 2 5/8-inches and 3 7/8-inches. It is a chestnut brown butterfly with two rows of white spots on a black forewing border. There are more white spots on the forewing apex in a scattered formation. The hindwing underside has black borders and veins, with white spots in two rows. The male's hindwing has a black scale patch.

Common Milkweed (*Asclepias syriaca*)
Jennifer Anderson @ USDA-NRCS PLANTS Database

Common Milkweed (*Asclepias syriaca*)

Plant Description: This perennial grows 18 to 36 inches high with pink, purple, or lilac flowers. Its blooms droop slightly and are in clusters. Bloom season is between June and August. Leaves are opposite and green in color.

Growing Guide: This milkweed prefers full sun but can grow in partial shade too. It likes a moist soil and can be propagated by seed with no pretreatment necessary.

Interesting Facts: The flower buds, seed pods, and leaves are edible. They need to be boiled and the water discarded, then reboiled to tend to the bitterness.

Warnings: Due to resinoids, the stem and leaf sap can be poisonous.

Southern Distribution: Alabama, Arkansas, Georgia, Kentucky, Louisiana, Mississippi, North Carolina, South Carolina, Tennessee, Virginia, and West Virginia.

Classification: Family *Asclepiadaceae* – Milkweed family

Genus *Asclepias* L. – milkweed

Species *Asclepias syriaca* L. – common milkweed

Butterflies and Moths Attracted: It is a larval host to the Monarch (*Danaus plexippus*) butterfly. The monarch has a G5, or secure, NatureServe Global Status and a large wingspan of 3 3/8-inches to 4 7/8-inches. Looking much like a viceroy, it has white spots on the apex and borders. Males are orange with black veins and borders and the females have orange-brown with black borders and blurry black veins. There are scent scales on the hindwing.

Monarch
(C) Mark Dreiling of Santee, CA

Butterflyweed (*Asclepias tuberosa*)
Larry Allain @ USDA-NRCS PLANTS Database

Butterflyweed (*Asclepias tuberosa*)

Also Known As: Butterfly Milkweed, Pleurisy Root, Orange Milkweed

Plant Description: Growing 1 1/2 feet to 2 feet tall, this perennial has bright orange or yellow-orange clusters of flowers. It grows bushy with alternate pointed leaves. Blooms will blossom between May and September.

Growing Guide: Plant this perennial in either full sun or partial shade. Soils should be well-drained, but it will tolerate wet or dry soils. It also tolerates drought. Propagate by seeds or root cuttings. Two-inch sections of taproot should be used for cuttings and seeds should be mature before sowing.

Interesting Facts: It was a folklore remedy for pleurisy, bronchitis, and diarrhea. First Nations People chewed the root for respiratory ailments while the root tea was drunk for diarrhea.

Warnings: This is not an edible plant and is toxic if eaten in large quantities. All parts of this milkweed have cardiac glycosides and resinoids that are toxic and can, upon ingesting, give the person symptoms of vomiting, spasms, weakness, and stupor.

Southern Distribution: Alabama, Arkansas, Florida, Georgia, Kentucky, Louisiana, Mississippi, North Carolina, South Carolina, Tennessee, Texas, Virginia, and West Virginia.

Classification: Family *Asclepiadaceae* – Milkweed family

Genus *Asclepias* L. – milkweed

Species *Asclepias tuberosa* L. – butterfly milkweed

Butterflies and Moths Attracted: It is a larval host the Monarch (*Danaus plexippus*) and Queen (*Danaus gilippus*) butterflies. The monarch has a G5, or secure, NatureServe Global Status and a large wingspan of 3 3/8-inches to 4 7/8-inches. Looking much like a viceroy, it has white spots on the apex and borders. Males are orange with black veins and borders and the females have orange-brown with black borders and blurry black veins. There are scent scales on the hindwing.

The Queen has a G5, or secure, NatureServe Global Status and a wingspan between 2 5/8-inches and 3 7/8-inches. It is a chestnut brown butterfly with two rows of white spots on a black forewing border. There are more white spots on the forewing apex in a scattered formation. The hindwing underside has black borders and veins, with white spots in two rows. The male's hindwing has a black scale patch.

Whorled Milkweed (*Asclepias verticillata*)

Also Known As: Eastern Whorled Milkweed

Plant Description: This single-stemmed plant grows 1 to 3 feet high with narrow leaves that are whorled. Green-white blooms are in clusters on the top of the stem. Flowers are small and arrive between May and September. It is unbranched.

Growing Guide: Whorled milkweed prefers full sun or partial shade with a dry soil. Propagate by seeds sown in the fall.

Interesting Facts: Even though the seeds germinate quickly, the plants usually will not bloom until the second year.

Warnings: This particular milkweed is one of the milkweeds that are most toxic to livestock. All parts are poisonous due to cardiac glycosides and resinoids.

Southern Distribution: Alabama, Arkansas, Florida, Georgia, Kentucky, Louisiana, Mississippi, North Carolina, South Carolina, Tennessee, Texas, Virginia, and West Virginia.

Classification: Family *Asclepiadaceae* – Milkweed family

Genus *Asclepias* L. – milkweed

Species *Asclepias verticillata* L. – whorled milkweed

Butterflies and Moths Attracted: It is a larval host to the Monarch (*Danaus plexippus*) butterfly. The monarch has a G5, or secure, NatureServe Global Status and a large wingspan of 3 3/8-inches to 4 7/8-inches. Looking much like a viceroy, it has white spots on the apex and borders. Males are orange with black veins and borders and the females have orange-brown with black borders and blurry black veins. There are scent scales on the hindwing.

Coastal Water-hyssop (*Bacopa monnieri*)
Larry Allain @ USDA-NRCS PLANTS Database

Coastal Water-hyssop (*Bacopa monnieri*)

Also Known As: Herb-of-Grace, Water Hyssop

Plant Description: Growing under a foot, there are small flowers and tiny oval leaves on this mat-forming aquatic plant. Flowers are bell-like, white with bluish or pinkish hues, and occur between April and September.

Growing Guide: This perennial prefers full sun or partial shade and wet or moist soil. Propagate by clump division.

Interesting Facts: This plant is used in Indian Ayurvedic medicine.

Southern Distribution: Alabama, Florida, Georgia, Louisiana, Mississippi, North Carolina, South Carolina, Texas, and Virginia.

Classification: Family *Scrophulariaceae* – Figwort family

Genus *Bacopa* Aubl. – waterhyssop

Species *Bacopa monnieri* (L.) Pennell – coastal water-hyssop

Butterflies and Moths Attracted: It is a larval host to the White Peacock (*Anartia jatrophae*) butterfly. The white peacock butterfly has a NatureServe Global Status of G5, or secure, and a wingspan of 2-inches to 2 3/4-inches. It is white with two rows of marginal crescents and light brown markings. There is a black spot on forewing and two on the hindwing. Summer butterflies are smaller and darker than their winter counterparts.

Blue Wild Indigo (*Baptisia australis*)
Clarence A. Rechenthin @ USDA-NRCS PLANTS Database

Blue Wild Indigo (*Baptisia australis*)

Also Known As: *Baptisia australis* var. *minor*, *Baptisia minor*, Blue False Indigo

Plant Description: Growing two to four feet high, this perennial has blue-purple flowers and divided leaves. Blooms are pea-like and arrive April through July. Flowers are in dense terminal spikes. It has a woody base and may break off at the ground level. Leaves turn a silver-gray in the fall.

Growing Guide: The blue wild indigo prefers full sun and a moist well-drained soil that is acidic to nearly neutral in pH. Propagate by seed or by division.

Interesting Facts: While today we realize it is a poisonous plant, it was once used by Native Americans as a toothache remedy and an anti-inflammatory.

Warnings: This plant is poisonous if ingested, despite its once use as a medicinal plant.

Southern Distribution: Alabama, Arkansas, Georgia, Kentucky, North Carolina, Tennessee, Texas, Virginia, and West Virgina.

Classification: Family *Fabaceae*– Pea family

Genus *Baptisia* Vent.– wild indigo

Species *Baptisia australis* (L.) R. Br.– blue wild indigo

Butterflies and Moths Attracted: It is a larval host to the Frosted Elfin (*Callophrys irus*) and the Wild Indigo Duskywing (*Erynnis baptisiae*).The frosted elfin has a G3, or vulnerable, NatureServe Global Status and a wingspan of 1-inch to 1 1/4-inches. It is a brown butterfly with a short hindwing tail. There is a long oval spot on the male's forewing edge. There is a black spot on the hindwing above the tail.

The wild indigo duskywing has a G5, or secure, NatureServe Global Status and a wingspan of 1 3/8-inches to 1 5/8-inches. A dark winged forewing upperside has an outer-half that is lighter in tone. There are orange-brown areas by the ends of cells. Females have scent scales on abdomen while males have yellow scent scales on the costal fold.

Horseflyweed (*Baptisia tinctoria*)

Also Known As: Yellow Wild Indigo

Plant Description: This perennial has gray-green leaves and hermaphrodite flowers. Blooming between May and September, the flowers are in yellow terminal clusters and pea-like.

Growing Guide: Grow this in full sun in a dry or moist soil. Soils should be well-drained and either acidic or neutral in pH. Propagate by seed or by division.

Interesting Facts: As a medicinal plant, it is used as a wound remedy when its roots are steeped in water. A root tea is a purgative. A root poultice is used for inflammation and toothaches. Horseflyweed washes are used for sprains, cuts, bruises, and other wounds.

Warnings: This plant is poisonous due to the toxic principles cytosine and baptisin.

Southern Distribution: Georgia, Kentucky, North Carolina, South Carolina, Tennessee, Virginia, and West Virginia.

Classification: Family *Fabaceae* – Pea family

Genus *Baptisia* Vent. – wild indigo

Species *Baptisia tinctoria* (L.) R. Br. – horseflyweed

Butterflies and Moths Attracted: It is a larval host to the Frosted Elfin (*Callophrys irus*) and Wild Indigo Duskywing (*Erynnis baptisiae*) butterflies. The frosted elfin has a G3, or vulnerable, NatureServe Global Status and a wingspan of 1-inch to 1 1/4-inches. It is a brown butterfly with a short hindwing tail. There is a long oval spot on the male's forewing edge. There is a black spot on the hindwing above the tail.

The wild indigo duskywing has a G5, or secure, NatureServe Global Status and a wingspan of 1 3/8-inches to 1 5/8-inches. A dark winged forewing upperside has an outer-half that is lighter in tone. There are orange-brown areas by the ends of cells. Females have scent scales on abdomen while males have yellow scent scales on the costal fold.

Bog Hemp (*Boehmeria cylindrica*)
Larry Allain @ USDA-NRCS PLANTS Database

Bog Hemp (*Boehmeria cylindrica*)

Also Known As: Smallspike False Nettle

Plant Description: Growing two to three feet high, this perennial has green simple leaves in an opposite pattern. Flowers are small and greenish, with blooms between July and October. They are in spikes and clustered.

Growing Guide: Bog hemp prefers to grow in any lighting with a moist soil. Propagate by seed or by division.

Interesting Facts: This species of the nettle family lacks stinging hairs and can be differentiated from the other member that lacks stinging hair (*Pilea pumila*, the Clearweed), in that it doesn't have a translucent stem.

Southern Distribution: Alabama, Arkansas, Florida, Georgia, Kentucky, Louisiana, Mississippi, North Carolina, South Carolina, Tennessee, Texas, Virginia, and West Virginia.

Classification: Family *Urticaceae*– Nettle family

Genus *Boehmeria* Jacq.– false nettle

Species *Boehmeria cylindrica* (L.) Sw.– bog hemp

Butterflies and Moths Attracted: It is a larval host for the Eastern Comma (*Polygonia comma*) and the Question Mark (*Polygonia interrogationis*). The eastern comma has a secure G5 NatureServe Global Status and a wingspan of 1 3/4-inches to 2 1/2-inches. It has a dark spotted brown-orange forewing upperside and a dark spot on the edge center. There are hindwing projections and a brown underside. Hindwing has a white or silver comma at both ends.

The question mark butterfly has a G5, or secure, NatureServe Global Status and a wingspan between 2 1/4-inches and 3-inches. It is red-orange with black spots and a hooked forewing. There is a light brown underside with a pearl-white question mark in center of the hindwing. Winter butterflies have a longer tail than summer butterflies and have a hindwing upperside that is more orange than the blacker summer form.

Winecup (*Callirhoe involucrata*)
Clarence A. Rechenthin @ USDA-NRCS PLANTS Database

Winecup (*Callirhoe involucrata*)

Also Known As: Purple Poppy Mallow

Plant Description: This perennial grows up to one foot high. It is a sprawling plant, with stems growing three feet long. Leaves are hairy, green, and rounded. Flowers are open in the mornings and closed in the evenings. Blooms are shaped like a chalice and occur between March and June. Typical flower colors are white, purple, or pink.

Growing Guide: Grow in full sun or partial shade with a moist or dry well-drained soil. Propagate by seed or softwood cuttings. Seed will germinate better after scarification. Sow seed in the fall. Take tip cuttings before the plant forms buds.

Interesting Facts: Winecup is a folklore remedy for several things. The roots can be dried, crushed, and burned to inhale for the common cold. Boiled roots make a tea that is drank for a pain remedy. These are old medicinal lore and should not be tried today.

Southern Distribution: Arkansas, Florida, Texas, and Virginia.

Classification: Family *Malvaceae* – Mallow family

Genus *Callirhoe* Nutt. – poppymallow

Species *Callirhoe involucrata* (Torr. & A. Gray) A. Gray – winecup

Butterflies and Moths Attracted: It is a larval host to the Gray Hairstreak (*Strymon melinus*) butterfly. The gray hairstreak has a secure rating, or G5, for its NatureServe Global Status and a wingspan between 7/8-inch and 1 3/8-inches. It is blue-gray with a red spot near the tail. There is one tail. The spring or fall variable of the butterfly is gray on the underside while the summer variable is pale gray. There is a white postmedian line that is bordered in orange.

Trumpet Creeper (*Campsis radicans*)
Larry Allain @ USDA-NRCS PLANTS Database

Trumpet Creeper (*Campsis radicans*)

Also Known As: Trumpet Vine, Cow Vine, *Bignonia radicans*, *Tecoma radicans*

Plant Description: Growing up to 35 feet, this woody vine has compound deciduous leaves and showy trumpet-like flowers. Leaves are dark green on top and lighter on the bottom. Flowers are waxy and bloom between June through September. Flowers can be red, orange, or yellow. Fruits are brown pods, 3 to 5 inches long.

Growing Guide: Plant a trumpet creeper in full sun with a well-drained nearly neutral in pH soil. Soil can be moist or dry. It is both cold and heat tolerant. Propagate by seed, root cuttings, and semi-hardwood cuttings. Cuttings should be 3 to 4 inches if semi-hardwood. Seed will need 1 to 2 months of cool stratification.

Interesting Facts: Because it grows rapidly and colonizes through suckers and layers, at one time the trumpet creeper was used as a means for erosion control.

Warnings: This may need mowing to help keep it in a defined area. It also can be a skin irritant from the plant's sap.

Southern Distribution: Alabama, Florida, Georgia, Kentucky, Louisiana, Mississippi, North Carolina, South Carolina, Tennessee, Texas, Virginia, and West Virginia.

Classification: Family *Bignoniaceae* – Trumpet-creeper family

Genus *Campsis* Lour. – campsis

Species *Campsis radicans* (L.) Seem. ex Bureau – trumpet creeper

Butterflies and Moths Attracted: It is a larval host to the Plebeian Sphinx (*Paratrea plebeja*). This moth has a NatureServe Global Status rank of G5, meaning that it is secure and not in danger of extinction. Its wingspan is between 2 3/8-inches to 3-inches. Plebeian sphinx moths are noted as having black and white markings on a gray wing.

Cutleaf Toothwort (*Cardamine concatenata*)
Jennifer Anderson @ USDA-NRCS PLANTS Database

Cutleaf Toothwort (*Cardamine concatenata*)

Also Known As: Pepper Root, *Dentaria laciniata*

Plant Description: Growing 6 to 12 inches high, this deciduous perennial has a cluster of flowers on its stem. Flowers are pink or white, four-petaled, and on a terminal cluster. Leaves are deeply divided and toothed. Flowers will bloom between March and May.

Growing Guide: Grow cutleaf toothwort in shade with a moist soil that is nearly neutral in pH. Propagate by root division or by seed.

Interesting Facts: The name 'toothwort' is from the underground stems having tooth-like projections.

Southern Distribution: Alabama, Arkansas, Florida, Georgia, Kentucky, Louisiana, Mississippi, North Carolina, South Carolina, Tennessee, Texas, Virginia, and West Virginia.

Classification: Family *Brassicaceae* – Mustard family

Genus *Cardamine* L. – bittercress

Species *Cardamine concatenata* (Michx.) Sw. – cutleaf toothwort

Butterflies and Moths Attracted: It is a larval host plant to the West Virginia White (*Pieris virginiensis*) butterfly. The West Virginia white butterfly has a G4, or apparently secure, rating from the NatureServe Global Status and a wingspan between 1 3/4-inches to 2 1/8-inches. It has whitish translucent wings. There is blurry brown or pale gray scaling on the veins on the underside to the hindwing.

Crinkleroot (*Cardamine diphylla*)

Also Known As: Two-leaved Toothwort, *Dentaria diphylla*

Plant Description: This perennial has paired leaves and clustered flowers, growing up to 16 inches tall. The foliage has deep dissected leaves and in 3 to 5 sections. Flowers are white or pink, loosely clustered, and bloom between March and June.

Growing Guide: Crinkleroot prefers partial to full shade conditions and a moist acidic soil. Propagate by rootstock division or by seeds. Division should happen when the plant is dormant and seeds should be sown after collection.

Warnings: This plant is in tolerant of shade.

Southern Distribution: Alabama, Arkansas, Georgia, Kentucky, Mississippi, North Carolina, South Carolina, Tennessee, Virginia, and West Virginia.

Classification: Family *Brassicaceae* – Mustard family

Genus *Cardamine* L. – bittercress

Species *Cardamine diphylla* (Michx.) Alph. Wood – crinkleroot

Butterflies and Moths Attracted: It is a larval host to the West Virginia White (*Pieris virginiensis*) butterfly. The West Virginia white butterfly has a G4, or apparently secure, rating from the NatureServe Global Status and a wingspan between 1 3/4-inches to 2 1/8-inches. It has whitish translucent wings. There is blurry brown or pale gray scaling on the veins on the underside to the hindwing.

Partridge Pea (*Chamaecrista fasciculata*)
Clarence A. Rechenthin @ USDA-NRCS PLANTS Database

Partridge Pea (*Chamaecrista fasciculata*)

Also Known As: Sensitive Plant, Sleeping Plant, *Chamaecrista fasciculata var. fasciculata, Cassia chamaecrista*

Plant Description: An annual, this will grow one to three feet tall with compound yellow-green leaves. Flowers are large and yellow and come from the leaf axil. Bloom season is between June and October. There is a pea like fruit.

Growing Guide: Plant this annual in full sun or partial shade with a well-drained soil. Soil can be moist or dry. Propagate by seed.

Interesting Facts: The seedpods are a food source for gamebirds and songbirds.

Warnings: The leaves of a partridge pea will fold up or collapse when touched. This is why it is called the sensitive plant.

Southern Distribution: Alabama, Arkansas, Florida, Georgia, Kentucky, Mississippi, North Carolina, South Carolina, Tennessee, Texas, Virginia, and West Virginia.

Classification: Family *Fabaceae* – Pea family

Genus *Chamaecrista* (L.) Moench – sensitive pea

Species *Chamaecrista fasciculata* (Michx.) Greene – partridge pea

Butterflies and Moths Attracted: It is a larval host to the Cloudless Sulphur (*Phoebis sennae*) and the Sleepy Orange (*Abaeis nicippe*) butterflies. The cloudless sulphur has a secure G5 NatureServe Global Status rating and a wingspan between 2 1/4-inches and 3 1/8-inches. Males are yellow with their hindwing's lower surface having 2 silver spots with pink edges. Females are white or yellow with black bordered wings. They too have a hindwing lower surface possessing 2 silver spots with pink edges.

The sleepy orange has a G5, or secure, NatureServe Global Status and a wingspan between 1 3/8-inches and 2 1/4-inches. Wings are orange with a black cell spot on the forewing. Females do not have defined borders but males have black outer and costal marginal borders. Summer has an orange-yellow underside and winter brings a red, brown, or tan underside.

Cloudless Sulphur
(C) Mark Dreiling of Santee, CA

Sleepy Orange
(C) Mark Dreiling of Santee, CA

White Turtlehead (*Chelone glabra*)
Robert H. Mohlenbrock @ USDA-NRCS PLANTS Database / USDA SCS. 1989. Midwest wetland flora: Field office illustrated guide to plant species. Midwest National Technical Center, Lincoln.

White Turtlehead (*Chelone glabra*)

Plant Description: Growing between one and four feet high, this erect stemmed perennial has white or lavender-white tubular flowers. Blooms look similar to a turtle's head, hence the name. Flowers are two-lipped and bloom between July and September. Foliage is opposite with elongated leaves.

Growing Guide: Plant a white turtlehead in any lighting with a wet or moist acidic soil. Propagate by seed, stem cuttings, or by root division. Seed will need cold-moist stratification for 6 weeks before sowing.

Interesting Facts: The name 'chelone' is Greek for tortoise and comes from the way the flowers look like turtleheads.

Southern Distribution: Alabama, Arkansas, Georgia, Kentucky, Mississippi, North Carolina, South Carolina, Tennessee, Virginia, and West Virginia.

Classification: Family *Scrophulariaceae* – Figwort family

Genus *Chelone* L. – turtlehead

Species *Chelone glabra* L. – white turtlehead

Butterflies and Moths Attracted: It is a larval host to the Baltimore Checkerspot (*Euphydryas phaeton*) butterfly. The Baltimore Checkerspot has a G4 NatureServe Global Status rank and a wingspan of 1 3/4-inches to 2 3/4-inches. It is a variable butterfly, but generally has black wings with red-orange outer margin crescents. Inward to the wing, there will be rows of white spots.

Lambsquarters (*Chenopodium album*)
Bill Summers @ USDA-NRCS PLANTS Database / USDA SCS. 1989. Midwest wetland flora: Field office illustrated guide to plant species. Midwest National Technical Center, Lincoln.

Lambsquarters (*Chenopodium album*)

USDA Native Status listed as both Native and Introduced

Plant Description: Growing up to 3 1/2 feet tall, this annual has clusters of green or brown flowers and simple leaves. Leaves are dull green with a dull gray hue to them. Bloom season is between June and October.

Growing Guide: This can grow in any lighting and soil type. Weed varieties that are non-native should be ripped up from the roots, while the native varieties can be propagated by seed.

Interesting Facts: Some varieties of this plant are native and some are introduced. Native varieties include 'var. missouriense' and 'var. striatum'.

Warnings: This plant has saponins, which can be toxic.

Southern Distribution: Alabama, Arkansas, Florida, Georgia, Kentucky, Louisiana, Mississippi, North Carolina, South Carolina, Tennessee, Texas, Virginia, and West Virginia.

Classification: Family *Chenopodiaceae* – Goosefoot family

Genus *Chenopodium* L. – goosefoot

Species *Chenopodium album* L. – lambsquarters

Butterflies and Moths Attracted: It is a larval host to the Western Pygmy-blue (*Brephidium exilis*) in the states of Lousisana, Arkansas, and Texas. It is also a larval host to the Common Sootywing (*Pholisora catullus*) butterfly. The western pygmy-blue has a secure G5 NatureServe Global Status and a wingspan between 1/2-inch and 3/4-inch. It is copper-brown with the bases a dull blue color. The hindwing is copper-brown on the underside with white fringe and white on the base next to 3 black spots.

With a G5 secure NatureServe Global Status, the common sootywing has a wingspan of 1-inch to 1 5/16-inches. It is black with a white spotted forewing. Females have a spotted row on the hindwing. Males have less white spots on the forewing. Hindwing is black.

Field Thistle (*Cirsium discolor*)

Plant Description: This biennial has small flowers arranged in a larger head that looks like a single flower. It is radially symmetrical and cupped by a green bract ring. Blooms should appear between June through September.

Growing Guide: Plant this thistle in full sun with a dry soil. It should be propagated by seed.

Interesting Facts: The seed of this plant is a favorite of the goldfinch bird.

Southern Distribution: Alabama, Arkansas, Georgia, Kentucky, Mississippi, North Carolina, Louisiana, South Carolina, Tennessee, Virginia, and West Virginia.

Classification: Family *Asteraceae* – Aster family

Genus *Cirsium* Mill. – thistle

Species *Cirsium discolor* (Muhl. ex Willd.) Spreng. – field thistle

Butterflies and Moths Attracted: It is a larval host to the Painted Lady (*Vanessa cardui*) butterfly. The painted lady is secure with a G5 NatureServe Global Status and has a wingspan between 2-inches and 2 7/8-inches. It has orange-brown wings with a darker base of the wings and an underside of black, brown, and gray. Undersides have four small eyespots. The forewing has a white edge bar and a black patch on apex. The hindwing has black spots in five rows and could have blue scales depending on butterfly.

Yellow Thistle (*Cirsium horridulum*)
Robert H. Mohlenbrock @ USDA-NRCS PLANTS Database / USDA SCS. 1991. Southern wetland flora: Field office guide to plant species. South National Technical Center, Fort Worth.

Yellow Thistle (*Cirsium horridulum*)

Plant Description: Growing 1 to 5 1/2 feet high, this branching plant has yellow or reddish-purple flowerheads. Leaves are spiny. Bloom season is between May through August.

Growing Guide: Grow this annual in full sun with a well-drained moist soil. It tolerates both poor soils and drought conditions. Propagate by seed.

Southern Distribution: Alabama, Arkansas, Florida, Georgia, Louisiana, Mississippi, North Carolina, South Carolina, Tennessee, Texas, and Virginia.

Classification: Family *Asteraceae* – Aster family

Genus *Cirsium* Mill. – thistle

Species *Cirsium horridulum* Michx. – yellow thistle

Butterflies and Moths Attracted: It is a larval host to the Little Metalmark (*Calephelis virginiensis*) butterfly. With a G4 apparently secure NatureServe Global Status, the little metalmark has a wingspan of 1/2-inch to 1-inch. This is a small rust-orange butterfly on the upperside with dark fringes. There is a bright orange color to the underside.

Swamp Thistle (*Cirsium muticum*)

Also Known As: *Carduus muticus, Cirsium bigelovii, Cirsium muticum var. monticola, Cirsium muticum var. subpinnatifidum*

Plant Description: This biennial can grow up to 8 feet high but is usually around 5 feet. Leaves are lobed and spaced wide on the stem. Flowers are deep purple or pink in flower heads about 1 1/2 inches wide. Blooms occur between July through September.

Growing Guide: Grow a swamp thistle in full sun or partial shade in wet or moist soils. Propagate by seed.

Southern Distribution: Alabama, Arkansas, Florida, Georgia, Kentucky, Louisiana, North Carolina, South Carolina, Tennessee, Texas, Virginia, and West Virginia.

Classification: Family *Asteraceae* – Aster family

Genus *Cirsium* Mill. – thistle

Species *Cirsium muticum* Michx. – swamp thistle

Butterflies and Moths Attracted: It is a larval host to the Swamp Metalmark (*Calephelis muticum*) butterfly. The swamp metalmark has a G4, or apparently secure, NatureServe Global Status and a wingspan between 15/16-inch and 1 3/16-inches. It is red-brown with light checkered fringes. The males will have a pointed forewing.

Rocky Mountain Beeplant (*Cleome serrulata*)

Also Known As: Waa, Skunk Weed

Plant Description: With erect leafy stems, the Rocky Mountain beeplant grows 4 to 5 feet high. It is an annual with compound leaves and red-purple, pink, or white flowers in racemes. Bloom season is between July and September. Seed capsules are slender.

Growing Guide: Grow this in full sun or partial shade with a dry well-drained soil. Propagate by seed. No pretreating is needed, but moist stratification can help.

Interesting Facts: Seeds are a food for doves. Seeds were also made into tortillas for early Spanish-Americans in times of drought.

Southern Distribution: Texas

Classification: Family *Capparaceae* – Caper family

Genus *Cleome* L. – spiderflower

Species *Cleome serrulata* Pursh – Rocky Mountain beeplant

Butterflies and Moths Attracted: It is a larval host to the Checkered White (*Pontia protodice*) butterfly. The checkered white has an apparently secure G4 NatureServe Global Status and a wingspan of 1 1/2-inches to 2 1/2-inches. Males have a black check pattern on the forewing upperside while the female is browner. There is a white hindwing, with pale checks on the male and yellow-tan areas on the female.

Hogwort (*Croton capitatus*)

Plant Description: This plant grows up to 36 inches high with alternate leaves and compact clusters of flowers. Blooms are white and occur between July through September. It will fruit with a 3-seeded capsule. Stems are hairy.

Growing Guide: Grow in full sun with a moist soil. Propagate by seed.

Interesting Facts: Doves and quail eat the seeds and are an important food source for the two.

Warnings: Even though it is very unpalatable due to bitterness, if ingested by livestock it can be toxic.

Southern Distribution: Alabama, Arkansas, Florida, Georgia, Kentucky, Louisiana, Mississippi, North Carolina, South Carolina, Tennessee, Texas, Virginia, and West Virginia.

Classification: Family *Euphorbiaceae* – Spurge family

Genus *Croton* L. – croton

Species *Croton capitatus* Michx. – hogwort

Butterflies and Moths Attracted: It is a larval host to the Goatweed Leafwing (*Anaea andria*) butterfly. The goatweed leafwing has a G5 secure NatureServe Global Status and a wingspan between 2 3/8-inches and 3 1/4-inches. Males are dull red in the summer with a short hindwing tail and a hooked forewing tip. Winter males have a longer tail, darker coloring, and a more hooked forewing. Females are light red with a yellow band. Winter females have a hooked forewing tip. The underside of both sexes looks like a dead leaf.

Prairie Tea (*Croton monanthogynus*)
Larry Allain @ USDA-NRCS PLANTS Database

Prairie Tea (*Croton monanthogynus*)

Also Known As: One-seed Croton

Plant Description: Growing 2 feet high and 3 feet wide, this has hairy stems and a fetid fragrance. Leaves are green above and whitish-green below, in an alternate form. Flowers are obscure, flowering between April and September. It will fruit in a capsule, typically having only one seed.

Growing Guide: Grow this annual in full sun with a dry poor soil. It is drought resistant. Propagate by seed.

Interesting Facts: Doves and quail eat the seeds and are an important food source for the two.

Southern Distribution: Alabama, Arkansas, Georgia, Kentucky, Louisiana, Mississippi, North Carolina, South Carolina, Tennessee, Texas, Virginia, and West Virginia.

Classification: Family *Euphorbiaceae* – Spurge family

Genus *Croton* L. – croton

Species *Croton monanthogynus* Michx. – prairie tea

Butterflies and Moths Attracted: It is a larval host to the Goatweed Leafwing (*Anaea andria*) butterfly. The goatweed leafwing has a G5 secure NatureServe Global Status and a wingspan between 2 3/8-inches and 3 1/4-inches. Males are dull red in the summer with a short hindwing tail and a hooked forewing tip. Winter males have a longer tail, darker coloring, and a more hooked forewing. Females are light red with a yellow band. Winter females have a hooked forewing tip. The underside of both sexes looks like a dead leaf.

Showy Tick Trefoil (*Desmodium canadense*)
Jennifer Anderson @ USDA-NRCS PLANTS Database

Showy Tick Trefoil (*Desmodium canadense*)

Plant Description: This plant has a bushy form and grows 2 to 6 feet tall. Its flowers are in terminal clusters, pink or rose-purple, and look like pea plant blooms. The bloom season is between June to September. It has hairy stems. Leaves are green and compound.

Growing Guide: This perennial prefers to grow in full sun with a moist soil. It tolerates acidity and dry soils. Propagate by seed.

Interesting Facts: Seeds will stick onto fur and clothing and this mechanism helps with the dispersal.

Southern Distribution: Texas, Virginia, and West Virginia.

Classification: Family *Fabaceae* – Pea family

Genus *Desmodium* Desv. – ticktrefoil

Species *Desmodium canadense* (L.) DC. – showy tick trefoil

Butterflies and Moths Attracted: It is a larval host to the Hoary Edge (*Achalarus lyciades*) and the Silver-spotted Skipper (*Epargyreus clarus*) butterflies. The hoary edge has a G5, or secure, NatureServe Global Status and a wingspan between 1 3/4-inches and 1 15/16-inches. It is dark brown with a gold band that is transparent on the forewing center. There are checkered fringes and a black-brown hindwing underside with a silver-white band.

With a secure NatureServe Global Status rating of G5, the silver-spotted skipper butterfly isn't near extinction. It has a wingspan of 1 3/4-inches to 2 5/8-inches. There are forewing gold spots and a hindwing with a silver band on this black or brown-winged butterfly. The hindwing of a silver-spotted skipper will be lobed.

Branched Dicliptera (*Dicliptera brachiata*)
Robert H. Mohlenbrock @ USDA-NRCS PLANTS Database / USDA SCS. 1991. Southern wetland flora: Field office guide to plant species. South National Technical Center, Fort Worth.

Branched Dicliptera (*Dicliptera brachiata*)

Also Known As: Branched Foldwing

Plant Description: Growing up to 24 inches tall, this branched plant has opposite 4-inch leaves and two-part flowers. Blooms are purple or pink and occur between July and October. Its fruits are brown capsules that encase the seeds.

Growing Guide: This perennial prefers partial shade and a moist well-drained soil. Propagate by seed.

Interesting Facts: It has a full sun tolerance however unless it is watered well and put in a rich soil, it runs the risk of getting sun bleached.

Warnings: Can reseed very well and may become a bit of a pest.

Southern Distribution: Alabama, Arkansas, Florida, Georgia, Kentucky, Louisiana, Mississippi, North Carolina, South Carolina, Tennessee, Texas, and Virginia.

Classification: Family *Acanthaceae* – Acanthus family

Genus *Dicliptera* Juss. – foldwing

Species *Dicliptera brachiata* (Pursh) Spreng. – branched dicliptera

Butterflies and Moths Attracted: It is a larval host to the Texan Crescent (*Anthanassa texana*) butterfly. The Texas crescent has a G4, or apparently secure, NatureServe Global Status and a wingspan between 1 1/4-inches and 1 7/8-inches. It is a white-spotted black butterfly with a rust color by the base of the wing. Cream spots are on the hindwing and there are indentions on the forewing outer margin.

Philadelphia Fleabane (*Erigeron philadelphicus*)
Jennifer Anderson @ USDA-NRCS PLANTS Database

Philadelphia Fleabane (*Erigeron philadelphicus*)

Also Known As: Fleabane Daisy

Plant Description: Growing 4 to 30 inches tall, this ray-flowered plant has hairy green leaves. Flowers are in clusters, and white or pink in color. Bloom season is between March and June. The petals of the flower are like threads, and can number more than 150 on the flower.

Growing Guide: Grow this short-lived perennial in partial shade with a well-drained moist soil. It does not tolerate full shade. Propagate by seed, with germination occurring after four weeks.

Interesting Facts: The name comes from the Greek words 'eri' for early and 'geron' for old man. It is a reference to its early flowering and appearance of having an "old man's beard".

Warnings: With sensitive-skinned individuals, this may cause contact dermatitis.

Southern Distribution: Alabama, Arkansas, Florida, Georgia, Kentucky, Louisiana, Mississippi, North Carolina, South Carolina, Tennessee, Texas, Virginia, and West Virginia.

Classification: Family *Asteraceae* – Aster family

Genus *Erigeron* L. – fleabane

Species *Erigeron philadelphicus* L. – Philadelphia fleabane

Butterflies and Moths Attracted: It is a larval host to the Northern Metalmark (*Calephelis borealis*) butterfly in the states of Arkansas, Virginia, West Virginia, and Kentucky, as well as a small portion of Texas and North Carolina. The northern metalmark has a NatureServe Global Status of G3, or vulnerable, and a wingspan between 1 1/8-inches and 1 1/4-inches. It is a brown butterfly with a dark band and orange borders. Males have a rounded forewing.

Bigleaf Aster (*Eurybia macrophylla*)

Also Known As: Large-leaf Wood-Aster, *Aster macrophyllus*

Plant Description: Growing up to 3 feet high, this perennial has basal heart-shaped leaves that are dark green. Flowers are in open clusters, white or violet in color, and occur between July and October.

Growing Guide: Plant a bigleaf aster in any lighting condition that has a moist or dry soil. Propagate by seed, division, or by softwood cuttings. Seed should have cold stratification before sowing.

Southern Distribution: Georgia, Kentucky, North Carolina, South Carolina, Tennessee, Virginia, and West Virginia.

Classification: Family *Asteraceae* – Aster family

Genus *Eurybia* (Cass.) Cass. – aster

Species *Eurybia macrophylla* (L.) Cass. – bigleaf aster

Butterflies and Moths Attracted: It is a larval host to the Pearl Crescent (*Phyciodes tharos*) butterfly. With a NatureServe Global Status rating of G5, or secure, the pearl crescent has a wingspan between 1 1/4-inches and 1 3/4-inches. It is a variable butterfly, but typically there is a black bordered orange upperside with fine black marks crossed over the post median. Males have black knobs on antennae. There is a dark marginal area to the hindwing underside with a light crescent.

Pearl Crescent
(C) Mark Dreiling of Santee, CA

Virginia Strawberry (*Fragaria virginiana*)

Also Known As: Wild Strawberry

Plant Description: Growing under a foot tall, this strawberry has a perennial growth and fibrous roots. There is a single trifoliate leaf on a hairy flower stalk. Flowers are small and have five petals, blooming between April and June. Fruits are red berries that are edible.

Growing Guide: Grow this perennial in full sun or partial shade with a dry soil. It can tolerate some acidity to the soil. Propagate by seed, stolon cuttings, or separating rooted plantlets.

Interesting Facts: This is one of the sweetest wild strawberries found.

Southern Distribution: Alabama, Arkansas, Florida, Georgia, Kentucky, Louisiana, Mississippi, North Carolina, South Carolina, Tennessee, Texas, Virginia, and West Virginia.

Classification: Family *Rosaceae* – Rose family

Genus *Fragaria* L. – strawberry

Species *Fragaria virginiana* Duchesne – Virginia strawberry

Butterflies and Moths Attracted: It is a larval host to the Grizzled Skipper (*Pyrgus centaureae*) in Kentucky, Tennessee, Virginia, and the Carolinas. It is also a larval host to the Gray Hairstreak (*Strymon melinus*) butterfly. The grizzled skipper has a G5, or secure, NatureServe Global Status and a wingspan between 1-inch and 1 5/16-inches. It has white checks on a gray-black upperside with checkered fringes. There is a white-checkered gray-brown or black hindwing underside. Veins are white on this butterfly. There will be forewing scent scales on the male.

The gray hairstreak has a secure rating, or G5, for its NatureServe Global Status and a wingspan between 7/8-inch and 1 3/8-inches. It is blue-gray with a red spot near the tail. There is one tail. The spring or fall variable of the butterfly is gray on the underside while the summer variable is pale gray. There is a white postmedian line that is bordered in orange.

American Licorice (*Glycyrrhiza lepidota*)

Also Known As: Wild Licorice

Plant Description: The American licorice plant grows erect up to 3 feet high. There are green compound leaves. It is a perennial with sticky-haired stems. Flowers are cream-colored and on a terminal spike. Fruits are spined, brown, and look like a cocklebur.

Growing Guide: American licorice prefers partial to full shade and moist soils. Propagate by stem cuttings, rhizome cuttings, and by seed. Seed should not be treated.

Interesting Facts: This has been a medicinal folklore plant used for diarrhea and upset stomach with a tea made from dried roots or leaves.

Warnings: Deer, gophers, and other small mammals eat multiple parts of this plant.

Southern Distribution: Arkansas, Texas, and Virginia

Classification: Family *Fabaceae* – Pea family

Genus *Glycyrrhiza* L. – licorice

Species *Glycyrrhiza lepidota* Pursh – American licorice

Butterflies and Moths Attracted: It is a larval host to the Silver-spotted Skipper (*Epargyreus clarus*) butterfly. With a secure NatureServe Global Status rating of G5, the silver-spotted skipper butterfly isn't near extinction. It has a wingspan of 1 3/4-inches to 2 5/8-inches. There are forewing gold spots and a hindwing with a silver band on this black or brown-winged butterfly. The hindwing of a silver-spotted skipper will be lobed.

Thinleaf Sunflower (*Helianthus decapetalus*)

Also Known As: Ten-petaled Sunflower, Pale Sunflower

Plant Description: This perennial grows 3 to 5 feet high, with light green, purple, or red-green stems. Leaves are glabrous and dark green on the upperside with a lighter color on the underside. Flowers are ray florets, yellow, and bloom for 1 to 1 1/2 months.

Growing Guide: This sunflower grows in any lighting with a moist soil, with a preference to growing in partial shade. Propagate by seed or by division of the rhizomes.

Interesting Facts: The name of the plant comes from three parts; the Greek word 'helios' that means sun, another Greek word 'anthos' that means flower, and the Latin word 'decapetalus' that means ten petals.

Southern Distribution: Alabama, Georgia, Kentucky, Louisiana, Mississippi, North Carolina, South Carolina, Tennessee, Virginia, and West Virginia.

Classification: Family *Asteraceae* – Aster family

Genus *Helianthus* L. – sunflower

Species *Helianthus decapetalus* L. – thinleaf sunflower

Butterflies and Moths Attracted: It is a larval host to the Silvery Checkerspot (*Chlosyne nycteis*) and Painted Lady (*Vanessa cardui*) butterflies. With a secure G5 NatureServe Global Status, the silvery checkerspot has a wingspan of 1 3/8-inches to 2-inches. It is a pale yellow-orange butterfly with dark markings and borders. There are white spots on the hindwing and a white crescent on the hindwing underside.

The painted lady is secure with a G5 NatureServe Global Status and has a wingspan between 2-inches and 2 7/8-inches. It has orange-brown wings with a darker base of the wings and an underside of black, brown, and gray. Undersides have four small eyespots. The forewing has a white edge bar and a black patch on apex. The hindwing has black spots in five rows and could have blue scales depending on butterfly.

Painted Lady
(C) Mark Dreiling of Santee, CA

Common Cowparsnip (*Heracleum maximum*)
Robert H. Mohlenbrock @ USDA-NRCS PLANTS Database / USDA SCS. 1989. Midwest wetland flora: Field office illustrated guide to plant species. Midwest National Technical Center, Lincoln.

Common Cowparsnip (*Heracleum maximum*)

Also Known As: Cow Parsnip, *Heracleum lanatum*

Plant Description: The common cowparsnip grows 3 to 10 feet tall with large leaves and small white flowers. There is a hollow stem that is stout and grooved. Blooming season is anytime between February and September.

Growing Guide: Grow the common cowparsnip in shade with a moist soil.

Interesting Facts: This plant looks very much like water hemlock (*Cicuta maculata*). However, water hemlock is poisonous while common cowparsnip is not.

Warnings: Those with sensitive skin may get contact dermatitis, a slight rash, when handling common cowparsnip and then exposing the area of contact to bright sunlight.

Southern Distribution: Georgia, Kentucky, North Carolina, Tennessee, Virginia, and West Virginia.

Classification: Family *Apiaceae* – Carrot family

Genus *Heracleum* L. – cowparsnip

Species *Heracleum maximum* Bartram – common cowparsnip

Butterflies and Moths Attracted: It is a larval host to the Black Swallowtail (*Papilio polyxenes*) butterfly. The black swallowtail has a secure G5 NatureServe Global Status and a wingspan of 3 1/4-inches to 4 1/4-inches. With near black uppersides there is an orange spot with an internal black spot on the hindwing's inner edge. Females have a blue band on the hindwing and a row of yellow spots. Males have a band that is yellow near the wing's edge.

Coral Honeysuckle (*Lonicera sempervirens*)
Robert H. Mohlenbrock @ USDA-NRCS PLANTS Database / USDA SCS. 1991. Southern wetland flora: Field office guide to plant species. South National Technical Center, Fort Worth.

Coral Honeysuckle (*Lonicera sempervirens*)

Also Known As: Trumpet Honeysuckle, Woodbine

Plant Description: Growing 3 to 20 feet long, this perennial semi-evergreen vine has smooth leaves and red tubular flowers. Flowers are in showy clusters while leaves are paired and glossy. Blooms will be between March and June. Fruits are red berries. Bark of the vine is papery, orange-brown in color, and exfoliating.

Growing Guide: Plant a coral honeysuckle in full sun or partial shade with a moist rich soil. It is tolerant of cold. Propagate by seed, softwood cuttings, layering, or semi-hardwood cuttings. Seed needs 2 to 3 months of cool stratification.

Interesting Facts: This has been used as a folklore remedy. Leaves have been dried and smoked to help asthma or chewed and then put on bee strings. Leaves can also be used for coughs and sore throats from a decoction.

Southern Distribution: Alabama, Arkansas, Georgia, Florida, Kentucky, Louisiana, Mississippi, North Carolina, South Carolina, Tennessee, Texas, Virginia, and West Virginia.

Classification: Family *Caprifoliaceae* – Honeysuckle family

Genus *Lonicera* L. – honeysuckle

Species *Lonicera sempervirens* L. – coral honeysuckle

Butterflies and Moths Attracted: It is a larval host to the Spring Azure (*Celastrina ladon*) and the Snowberry Clearwing (*Hemaris diffinis*). The spring azure has an apparent secure rating on NatureServe Global Status with a G4 rating. Its wingspan is between 7/8-inch and 1 3/8-inches. It has an upperside of a blue forewing and a gray-white underside.

The snowberry clearwing is secure, with a G5 NatureServe Global Status ranking. There is a 1 1/4-inch to 2-inch wingspan and it has a wide variety of looks, but typically looks like a bumblebee with clear wings.

Sundial Lupine (*Lupinus perennis*)

Also Known As: Wild Lupine

Plant Description: This lupine has one to two foot stems and purple, white, pink, or blue clusters of flowers. Leaves are compound and palmately divided. Bloom season is usually between May and June.

Growing Guide: Grow this perennial in full sun or partial shade with a dry soil that is acidic or nearly neutral in pH. Soil should be well-drained. Propagate by seed sown fresh or seed that has had scarification and then a 10-day moist stratification.

Interesting Facts: The sundial lupine can enhance soil's fertility by fixing nitrogen in the atmosphere to a useable form.

Warnings: The seeds of this plant are poisonous when ingested due to alkaloids such as anagyrine, sparteine, hydroxylupanine, and lupinine.

Southern Distribution: Alabama, Florida, Georgia, Kentucky, Mississippi, North Carolina, South Carolina, Texas, Virginia, and West Virginia.

Classification: Family *Fabaceae* – Pea family

Genus *Lupinus* L. – lupine

Species *Lupinus perennis* L. – sundial lupine

Butterflies and Moths Attracted: It is a larval host to the Frosted Elfin (*Callophrys irus*) and the Wild Indigo Duskywing (*Erynnis baptisiae*) butterflies. The frosted elfin has a G3, or vulnerable, NatureServe Global Status and a wingspan of 1-inch to 1 1/4-inches. It is a brown butterfly with a short hindwing tail. There is a long oval spot on the male's forewing edge. There is a black spot on the hindwing above the tail.

The wild indigo duskywing has a G5, or secure, NatureServe Global Status and a wingspan of 1 3/8-inches to 1 5/8-inches. A dark winged forewing upperside has an outer-half that is lighter in tone. There are orange-brown areas by the ends of cells. Females have scent scales on abdomen while males have yellow scent scales on the costal fold.

Common Moonseed (*Menispermum canadense*)

Plant Description: This native vine is woody, with simple leaves and blue fruits. Foliage is alternate on the vine. There are clusters of green-white flowers, blooming between June and July. Fruits are grape-like in appearance, each having a single crescent-shaped flat seed.

Growing Guide: It prefers to grow in any lighting condition with a moist soil. Propagate by division, cuttings, or by seed.

Interesting Facts: The Native Americans used a *Chondodendron tomentosum*, a member of the same family of plants, as arrow poison and has both anesthetic and muscle relaxing properties.

Warnings: This is a poisonous plant with highly toxic, possibly fatal, fruit.

Southern Distribution: Alabama, Arkansas, Florida, Georgia, Kentucky, Mississippi, North Carolina, South Carolina, Tennessee, Texas, Virginia, and West Virginia.

Classification: Family *Menispermaceae*– Moonseed family

Genus *Menispermum* L.– moonseed

Species *Menispermum canadense* L.– common moonseed

Butterflies and Moths Attracted: It is a larval host to the Variegated Fritillary (*Euptoieta claudia*). The variegated fritillary is secure with a G5 NatureServe Global Status and has a wingspan of 1 3/4-inches to 3 1/8-inches. Black spotted margins adorn an orange-brown wing with dark veins. There is a slight scallop to the hindwing and the underside is mottled.

Allegheny Monkeyflower (*Mimulus ringens*)

Also Known As: Square-stemmed Monkeyflower

Plant Description: With some plants reaching 4 feet high, typically this flower grows from 1 to 3 feet. It has an upright form with two-lipped flowers in a blue-purple color, resembling a snapdragon. Blooms are asymmetrical and arrive between June and September. Leaves are opposite and green.

Growing Guide: This perennial prefers full sun or partial shade conditions and a moist to wet soil. Propagate by seeds or by dividing the rhizomes.

Interesting Facts: Part of this plant's name is from the Latin 'mimus' which means buffoon.

Southern Distribution: Alabama, Arkansas, Georgia, Kentucky, Louisiana, Mississippi, North Carolina, South Carolina, Tennessee, Texas, Virginia, West Virginia.

Classification: Family *Scrophulariaceae* – Figwort family

Genus *Mimulus* L. – monkeyflower

Species *Mimulus ringens* L. – Allegheny monkeyflower

Butterflies and Moths Attracted: It is a larval host to the Baltimore Checkerspot (*Euphydryas phaeton*) and Common Buckeye (*Junonia coenia*) butterflies. The Baltimore Checkerspot has a G4 NatureServe Global Status rank and a wingspan of 1 3/4-inches to 2 3/4-inches. It is a variable butterfly, but generally has black wings with red-orange outer margin crescents. Inward to the wing, there will be rows of white spots.

The common buckeye butterfly has a G5, or secure, NatureServe Global Status and a wingspan of 1 5/8-inches to 2 3/4-inches. It is brown with two eyespots and two orange cell bars on the forewing and two eyespots in the hindwing. It has a brown or tan

hindwing underside in the summer and rose-red in the fall.

Common Buckeye
(C) Mark Dreiling of Santee, CA

Virginia Creeper (*Parthenocissus quinquefolia*)
Larry Allain @ USDA-NRCS PLANTS Database

Virginia Creeper (*Parthenocissus quinquefolia*)

Plant Description: This trailing vine grows 3 to 40 feet with green deciduous leaves and clusters of tiny flowers. Leaves are in groups of five and turn red, purple, or mauve in the fall. Flowers are greenish in color and fruits are bluish. Blooms arrive from May to June.

Growing Guide: Grow a Virginia creeper in any lighting with a moist well-drained soil. It is both cold and heat tolerant. Propagate by seed, hardwood cuttings, layering, or semi-hardwood cuttings. Seed should be sown in the fall if fresh or cold moist stratify for 2 months if sown in spring.

Interesting Facts: Many types of birds use this plant throughout the winter for both food and as a cover. It also is the other half of the poison ivy rhyme "Leaves of three, let it be; Leaves of five, let it thrive". Poison ivy has three-leaf groups while Virginia creeper has five-leaf groups.

Warnings: The berries contain oxalic acid and the plant tissue has raphides. Berries are poisonous and can give symptoms of nausea, diarrhea, headache, bloody vomit, and drowsiness if ingested. Plant tissue can irritate some sensitive skin.

Southern Distribution: Alabama, Arkansas, Florida, Georgia, Kentucky, Louisiana, Mississippi, North Carolina, South Carolina, Tennessee, Texas, Virginia, and West Virginia.

Classification: Family *Vitaceae* – Grape family

Genus *Parthenocissus* Planch. – creeper

Species *Parthenocissus quinquefolia* (L.) Planch. – Virginia creeper

Butterflies and Moths Attracted: It is a larval host to the Virginia Creeper Sphinx Moth (*Darapsa myron*), Abbotts Sphinx Moth (*Sphecodina abbottii*), Pandorus Sphinx Moth (*Eumorpha pandorus*), and the White-lined Sphinx Moth (*Hyles lineata*). The Virginia creeper sphinx has a G5 NatureServe Global Status and is secure. It has a wingspan of 1 3/4-inches to 2 9/16-inches. It has a dark brown to yellow-gray upperside and may have a dark rectangle on the costal margin. The top of the hindwing is a pale orange shade. Abbotts Sphinx is secure with a G5 NatureServe Global Status and a wingspan of 2-inches to 2 3/4-inches. They have scalloped wing margins, dark brown forewing tops and light brown bands. The hindwing is yellow and has a wide black section on its outer margin.

Pandorus Sphinx has a G5 NatureServe Global Status, a wingspan between 3 1/4-inches and 4 1/2-inches, and a green or olive tinted light brown upperside. There are pink streaked vein ends on forewing and dark green on the base until it reaches a dark square mark. The underside to the moth can be pale brown or yellow-green.

White-lined Sphinx has a NatureServe Global Status of G5, or secure, and a wingspan of 2 7/16-inches to 3 9/16-inches. With a white streaks on veins and a narrow tan band, the forewing upperside is dark olive brown. It has a black upperside on the hindwing and a pink-red median band.

Purple Passionflower (*Passiflora incarnata*)
Larry Allain @ USDA-NRCS PLANTS Database

Purple Passionflower (*Passiflora incarnata*)

Also Known As: Maypop, Apricot Vine

Plant Description: This perennial vine grows up to 25 feet with lavender flowers and deciduous leaves. Leaves are dark green on the topside and whiter on the bottom. Fruit is a yellow-orange berry that is edible. Blooms arrive between April and September. It has hair-like wavy fringed petals and sepals.

Growing Guide: Plant a purple passionflower in full sun or partial shade with a moist or dry soil. It is both cold and heat tolerant. Propagate by seeds or by cuttings. Seeds should be cleaned before sowing.

Interesting Facts: This was a Native American folklore remedy. Its leaves were crushed for poultices used for cuts and bruises. Teas were brewed with the leaves for insomnia and nerves. Roots were made into a poultice for earaches, cuts, and inflammation.

Purple Passionflower was named in part to the crucifixion story with 10 petal-like parts for the disciples (without Judas and Peter) and five stamens to represent the wounds received.

Southern Distribution: Alabama, Arkansas, Florida, Georgia, Kentucky, Mississippi, Louisiana, South Carolina, North Carolina, Tennessee, Texas, Virginia, and West Virginia.

Classification: Family *Passifloraceae* – Passion-flower family

Genus *Passiflora* L. – passionflower

Species *Passiflora incarnata* L. – purple passionflower

Butterflies and Moths Attracted: It is a larval host to the Zebra Heliconian (*Heliconius charithonia*), Gulf Fritillary (*Agraulis vanillae*), Variegated Fritillary (*Euptoieta claudia*), and the Banded Hairstreak (*Satyrium calanus*). The zebra heliconian has a NatureServe Global Status rating of G5, or secure, and a wingspan between 2 3/4-inches to 4-inches. It has a black body with long yellow stripes that are narrow.

The gulf fritillary has a NatureServe Global Status rating of G5, or secure, and a wingspan between 2 1/2-inches to 3 3/4-inches. There are bright orange wings marked with black on the upperside and three white dots lined with black on the forewing. On a brown underside there are long silver spots.

The variegated fritillary is secure with a G5 NatureServe Global Status and has a wingspan of 1 3/4-inches to 3 1/8-inches. Black spotted margins adorn an orange-brown wing with dark veins. There is a slight scallop to the hindwing and the underside is mottled.

The banded hairstreak has a NatureServe Global Status of G5, secure, and a wingspan of one-inch to 1 1/2-inches wide. There is a short and a long tail on the brown hindwing. Underside is darker with dark colored dashes with white edges. There is a blue tail spot and some orange near the tailspot.

Gulf Fritillary
(C) Mark Dreiling of Santee, CA

Yellow Passion Vine (*Passiflora lutea*)
Robert H. Mohlenbrock @ USDA-NRCS PLANTS Database / USDA SCS. 1991. Southern wetland flora: Field office guide to plant species. South National Technical Center, Fort Worth.

Yellow Passion Vine (*Passiflora lutea*)

Also Known As: Yellow Passionflower

Plant Description: Growing up to 15 feet long, this perennial vine has green-yellow flowers and purple or black berries. The foliage is wide and lobed, turning yellow in the fall. Bloom season is between May and September.

Growing Guide: Grow a yellow passion vine in partial shade with a moist soil. Propagate by seed or by layering.

Southern Distribution: Alabama, Arkansas, Florida, Georgia, Kentucky, Louisiana, Mississippi, North Carolina, South Carolina, Tennessee, Texas, Virginia, and West Virginia.

Classification: Family *Passifloraceae* – Passion-flower family

Genus *Passiflora* L. – passionflower

Species *Passiflora lutea* L. – yellow passionflower

Butterflies and Moths Attracted: It is a larval host to the Julia Heliconian (*Dryas julia*), Zebra Heliconian (*Heliconius charithonia*) butterfly and the Gulf Fritillary (*Agraulis vanillae*) butterfly. Julia heliconian is a G5 secure butterfly with its NatureServe Global Status and has a wingspan between 3 1/4-inches and 3 5/8-inches. It has enlongated forewings, with females having a dull orange upperside and underside and males having a bright orange upperside and underside. Females have more black markings than a male, with the male having an outer marginal black border on hindwing.

The zebra heliconian has a NatureServe Global Status rating of G5, or secure, and a wingspan between 2 3/4-inches to 4-inches. It has a black body with long yellow stripes that are narrow.

The gulf fritillary has a NatureServe Global Status rating of G5, or secure, and a wingspan between 2 1/2-inches to 3 3/4-inches. There are bright orange wings marked with black on the upperside and three white dots lined with black on the forewing. On a brown underside there are long silver spots.

Hairy Beardtongue (*Penstemon hirsutus*)

Plant Description: These hairy-stemmed flowers grow 16 to 24 inches high. There are oblong green leaves on the erect stem. Flowers are in clusters, on stalks, and are trumpet-like lavender blooms. They are slender and have white lips. Blooms can appear between June and July.

Growing Guide: This perennial grows well in full sun or partial shade and with a dry well-drained soil. Propagate by seed after a period of cold stratification.

Interesting Facts: This particular beardtongue is easy to identify over others due to its stem's hairy down.

Southern Distribution: Alabama, Kentucky, Tennessee, Virginia, and West Virginia.

Classification: Family *Scrophulariaceae* – Figwort family

Genus *Penstemon* Schmidel – beardtongue

Species *Penstemon hirsutus* (L.) Willd. – hairy beardtongue

Butterflies and Moths Attracted: It is a food source for the Baltimore Checkerspot (*Euphydryas phaeton*) butterfly. The Baltimore Checkerspot has a G4 NatureServe Global Status rank and a wingspan of 1 3/4-inches to 2 3/4-inches. It is a variable butterfly, but generally has black wings with red-orange outer margin crescents. Inward to the wing, there will be rows of white spots.

Texas Frogfruit (*Phyla nodiflora*)
Larry Allain @ USDA-NRCS PLANTS Database

Texas Frogfruit (*Phyla nodiflora*)

Also Known As: Turkey Tangle Frogfruit, Frogfruit, *Phyla incisa*

Plant Description: Growing under a foot tall, this groundcover has semi-evergreen leaves and verbena-like blooms. Leaves are green and turn purplish or reddish in the winter. Flowers are white and bloom between May and October.

Growing Guide: Plant a Texas frogfruit in full sun or partial shade with moist or dry soil. It is flood, drought, and heat tolerant but goes dormant through a hard winter. Propagate by root division and by cuttings.

Southern Distribution: Alabama, Arkansas, Florida, Georgia, Kentucky, Louisiana, Mississippi, North Carolina, South Carolina, Texas, and Virginia.

Classification: Family *Verbenaceae* – Verbena family

Genus *Phyla* Lour. – frogfruit

Species *Phyla nodiflora* (L.) Greene – Texas frogfruit

Butterflies and Moths Attracted: It is a larval host to the Phaon Crescent (*Phyciodes phaon*), the Common Buckeye (*Junonia coenia*), and the White Peacock (*Anartia* *jatrophae*) butterflies. With a G5 secure NatureServe Global Status, the Phaon crescent has a wingspan between 1-inch to 1 1/2-inches. The butterfly is dark orange and black with a cream band and cream or yellow-tinted hindwing underside.

The common buckeye butterfly has a G5, or secure, NatureServe Global Status and a wingspan of 1 5/8-inches to 2 3/4-inches. It is brown with two eyespots and two orange cell bars on the forewing and two eyespots in the hindwing. It has a brown or tan hindwing underside in the summer and rose-red in the fall.

The white peacock butterfly has a NatureServe Global Status of G5, or secure, and a wingspan of 2-inches to 2 3/4-inches. It is white with two rows of marginal crescents and light brown markings. There is a black spot on forewing and two on the hindwing. Summer butterflies are smaller and darker than their winter counterparts.

Blunt-leaf Rabbit-tobacco (*Pseudognaphalium obtusifolium ssp. obtusifolium*)
Larry Allain @ USDA-NRCS PLANTS Database

Blunt-leaf Rabbit-tobacco (*Pseudognaphalium obtusifolium ssp. obtusifolium*)

Also Known As: Sweet Everlasting, Rabbit-tobacco, *Gnaphalium obtusifolium*

Plant Description: The blunt-leaf rabbit-tobacco grows 1 to 2 1/2 feet tall with erect woolly stems and narrow leaves. Flowers are small, with a white color that changes to brown. Bloom season is between August and October.

Growing Guide: This annual prefers full sun and a soil that has sand or silt. It will tolerate some shade. Propagate by seed.

Warnings: Seed will need light to be able to germinate.

Southern Distribution: Alabama, Arkansas, Florida, Georgia, Kentucky, Louisiana, Mississippi, North Carolina, South Carolina, Tennessee, Texas, Virginia, and West Virginia.

Classification: Family *Asteraceae* – Aster family

Genus *Pseudognaphalium* Kirp. – cudweed

Species *Pseudognaphalium obtusifolium* (L.) Hilliard & B.L. Burtt – rabbit-tobacco

Subspecies *Pseudognaphalium obtusifolium* (L.) Hilliard & B.L. Burtt *ssp. obtusifolium* –

blunt-leaf rabbit-tobacco

Butterflies and Moths Attracted: It is a larval host to the American Lady (*Vanessa virginiensis*) butterfly. The American lady has a NatureServe Global Status of G5, or secure, and a wingspan between 1 3/4-inches and 2 5/8-inches. There is brown, orange, and yellow in an uneven form on the upperside. A black patch and orange area with a white dot is on the forewing. There are two large eyespots on the hindwing's underside.

Black-eyed Susan (*Rudbeckia hirta*)

Also Known As: Common Black-eyed Susan, Brown-eyed Susan

Plant Description: Growing 1 to 2 feet tall with bright yellow daisy-like flowers, this wildflower has dark centers. They are single flowers and not in clusters. Leaves are green and oval, covered with hair. Stems are rough and hairy. Flowers bloom between June and October.

Growing Guide: Plant this biennial plant in any lighting from full sun to full shade and in moist to dry acidic well-drained soil. It can be propagated by seed that has been stratified prior to sowing. It is drought tolerant.

Interesting Facts: Native Americans have used this plant for snakebites, swelling, earaches, and colds.

Warnings: Without competition, this *Rudbeckia* can be aggressive when in perfect conditions.

Southern Distribution: Alabama, Arkansas, Florida, Georgia, Kentucky, Louisiana, Mississippi, North Carolina, South Carolina, Tennessee, Texas, Virginia, and West Virginia.

Classification: Family *Asteraceae* – Aster family

Genus *Rudbeckia* L. – coneflower

Species *Rudbeckia hirta* L. – blackeyed Susan

Butterflies and Moths Attracted: It is a larval host to the Bordered Patch (*Chlosyne lacinia*) and the Gorgone Checkerspot (*Chlosyne gorgone*) butterflies. The bordered patch has a G5, or secure, NatureServe Global Status and a wingspan between 1 3/8-

inches and 2-inches. It is a variable butterfly with black wings and an orange or cream band and spots. The hindwing is black with yellow or cream bands spots; white on the postmedian and cream ones marginally.

The Gorgone checkerspot has a G4, or apparently secure, NatureServe Global Status and a wingspan of 1 1/4-inches to 1 3/4-inches. It is orange with black areas on the upperside and a row of black spots on the hindwing. The hindwing underside has white chevrons and brown and white zigzag bands.

Sidebeak Pencilflower (*Stylosanthes biflora*)
Larry Allain @ USDA-NRCS PLANTS Database

Sidebeak Pencilflower (*Stylosanthes biflora*)

Plant Description: This perennial grows up to 18 inches high with alternate leaves and small flowers. Flowers may be single blooms or in tiny clusters. Leaves are narrow and compound. Fruits are two-segmented pods. Bloom season is between May and September.

Growing Guide: This plant prefers being in full sun or partial shade with an acidic soil. Propagate by seed.

Interesting Facts: Native Americans used the plant for female troubles. They steeped the roots into a beverage and had the afflicted woman drink from it.

Southern Distribution: Alabama, Florida, Georgia, Kentucky, Mississippi, North Carolina, South Carolina, Tennessee, Texas, Virginia, and West Virginia.

Classification: Family *Fabaceae* – Pea family

Genus *Stylosanthes* Sw. – pencilflower

Species *Stylosanthes biflora* (L.) Britton, Sterns & Poggenb. – sidebeak pencilflower

Butterflies and Moths Attracted: It is a larval host to the Barred Yellow (*Eurema daira*) butterfly. The barred yellow has a NatureServe Global Status rank of G5, or secure, and a wingspan of 1 1/4-inches to 1 5/8-inches. Males have a yellow forewing upperside with an inner black bar and a black patch at the apex. Females are white or yellow with a black patch on the hindwing and a gray-black apex on forewing. In summer they are smaller and the hindwing underside is white. The hindwing in winter is tan or red with two black spots.

White Heath Aster (*Symphyotrichum ericoides var. ericoides*)
Clarence A. Rechenthin @ USDA-NRCS PLANTS Database

White Heath Aster (*Symphyotrichum ericoides var. ericoides*)

Also Known As: White Aster, Heath Aster, White Prairie Aster, *Aster ericoides, Aster multiflorus*

Plant Description: Growing up to 3 feet high, this perennial has clustered white ray flowers and health-like leaves. It has a bushy form and is grayish in hue. Bloom season is between September and November.

Growing Guide: Grow a white heath aster in full sun with a dry soil. It can be propagated by division, or by seed. Seed will need dry stratification to germinate, and rhizome division is the easiest form of propagation.

Interesting Facts: Many of the *Aster ericoides* that are sold are not native to the United States and are derivatives of the European asters.

Warnings: At the time of flowering, the lower stem leaves will die back.

Southern Distribution: Arkansas, Mississippi, Tennessee, Texas, Virginia, and West Virginia.

Classification: Family *Asteraceae* – Aster family

Genus *Symphyotrichum* Nees – aster

Species *Symphyotrichum ericoides* (L.) G.L. Nesom – white heath aster

Variety *Symphyotrichum ericoides* (L.) G.L. Nesom *var. ericoides* – white heath aster

Butterflies and Moths Attracted: It is a larval host to the Pearl Crescent (*Phyciodes tharos*) butterfly. With a NatureServe Global Status rating of G5, or secure, the pearl crescent has a wingspan between 1 1/4-inches and 1 3/4-inches. It is a variable butterfly, but typically there is a black bordered orange upperside with fine black marks crossed over the post median. Males have black knobs on antennae. There is a dark marginal area to the hindwing underside with a light crescent.

Smooth Blue Aster (*Symphyotrichum laeve var. laeve*)

Also Known As: Smooth Aster, *Aster laevis*

Plant Description: With 2- to 4-foot high stems, this plant has dark green leaves and a plethora of blooms. Leaves are smooth on the upperside and coarse underneath. Stems are stout and flowers are pale lavender with yellow centers. Bloom season is between August and October. The flowers are on open heads on top of the stems.

Growing Guide: Grow in full sun with a dry soil. Propagate by seed, softwood cuttings, or rhizome division. Seed should be sown in the fall. If sowing in the spring, it requires stratification.

Southern Distribution: Alabama, Arkansas, Georgia, Kentucky, Louisiana, Mississippi, North Carolina, South Carolina, Tennessee, Virginia, and West Virginia.

Classification: Family *Asteraceae* – Aster family

Genus *Symphyotrichum* Nees – aster

Species *Symphyotrichum laeve* (L.) A. Löve & D. Löve – smooth blue aster

Variety *Symphyotrichum laeve* (L.) A. Löve & D. Löve *var. laeve* – smooth blue aster

Butterflies and Moths Attracted: It is a larval host to the Pearl Crescent (*Phyciodes tharos*) butterfly. With a NatureServe Global Status rating of G5, or secure, the pearl crescent has a wingspan between 1 1/4-inches and 1 3/4-inches. It is a variable butterfly, but typically there is a black bordered orange upperside with fine black marks crossed over the post median. Males have black knobs on antennae. There is a dark marginal area to the hindwing underside with a light crescent.

Calico Aster (*Symphyotrichum lateriflorum var. lateriflorum*)
Robert H. Mohlenbrock @ USDA-NRCS PLANTS Database / USDA SCS. 1989. Midwest wetland flora: Field office illustrated guide to plant species. Midwest National Technical Center, Lincoln.

Calico Aster (*Symphyotrichum lateriflorum var. lateriflorum*)

Also Known As: *Aster lateriflorus*

Plant Description: Growing up to 3 feet high, this ray-flowered plant has green oval leaves. Blooms are white or purplish in loose clusters, typically on one side of the branches. Flowers will bloom between August and October.

Growing Guide: Grow this perennial in full sun with a moist soil. Propagate by cuttings or by seed.

Southern Distribution: Alabama, Arkansas, Florida, Georgia, Kentucky, Louisiana, Mississippi, North Carolina, South Carolina, Tennessee, Texas, Virginia, and West Virginia.

Classification: Family *Asteraceae* – Aster family

Genus *Symphyotrichum* Nees – aster

Species *Symphyotrichum lateriflorum* (L.) A. Löve & D. Löve – calico aster

Variety *Symphyotrichum lateriflorum* (L.) A. Löve & D. Löve *var. lateriflorum* – calico aster

Butterflies and Moths Attracted: It is a larval host to the Pearl Crescent (*Phyciodes tharos*) butterfly. With a NatureServe Global Status rating of G5, or secure, the pearl crescent has a wingspan between 1 1/4-inches and 1 3/4-inches. It is a variable butterfly, but typically there is a black bordered orange upperside with fine black marks crossed over the post median. Males have black knobs on antennae. There is a dark marginal area to the hindwing underside with a light crescent.

New England Aster (*Symphyotrichum novae-angliae*)
Jennifer Anderson @ USDA-NRCS PLANTS Database

New England Aster (*Symphyotrichum novae-angliae*)

Also Known As: New England American-aster, *Aster novae-angliae*

Plant Description: Growing up to six feet tall, this perennial has green leaves and showy flowers. Blooms are variable in color with a yellow-orange center. Flowering season is between August and October, with flowers appearing at the end of the branches. Leaves are hairy and are densely packed.

Growing Guide: Grow the New England aster in partial shade and moist acidic soil. Propagate by seed, softwood cuttings, or division. Seed require cold-moist stratification for three months.

Warnings: This can become aggressive.

Southern Distribution: Alabama, Arkansas, Georgia, Kentucky, Mississippi, North Carolina, South Carolina, Tennessee, Virginia, and West Virginia.

Classification: Family *Asteraceae* – Aster family

Genus *Symphyotrichum* Nees – aster

Species *Symphyotrichum novae-angliae* (L.) G.L. Nesom – New England aster

Butterflies and Moths Attracted: It is a larval host to the Pearl Crescent (*Phyciodes tharos*) butterfly. With a NatureServe Global Status rating of G5, or secure, the pearl crescent has a wingspan between 1 1/4-inches and 1 3/4-inches. It is a variable butterfly, but typically there is a black bordered orange upperside with fine black marks crossed over the post median. Males have black knobs on antennae. There is a dark marginal area to the hindwing underside with a light crescent.

Wavyleaf Aster (*Symphyotrichum undulatum*)

Also Known As: *Aster undulatus*

Plant Description: With alternate slightly-toothed leaves and ray flowers, this perennial grows up to 3 feet tall. Flowers are light blue or light violet, occurring between August and November. Stems are rough and stiff.

Growing Guide: This perennial prefers to grow in full sun areas and in dry soil. Propagate by seed.

Interesting Facts: The plants different varieties differ only by their leaf outline.

Southern Distribution: Alabama, Florida, Georgia, Kentucky, Louisiana, Mississippi, North Carolina, South Carolina, Tennessee, Virginia, and West Virginia.

Classification: Family *Asteraceae* – Aster family

Genus *Symphyotrichum* Nees – aster

Species *Symphyotrichum undulatum* (L.) G.L. Nesom – wavyleaf aster

Butterflies and Moths Attracted: It is a larval host to the Pearl Crescent (*Phyciodes tharos*) butterfly. With a NatureServe Global Status rating of G5, or secure, the pearl crescent has a wingspan between 1 1/4-inches and 1 3/4-inches. It is a variable butterfly, but typically there is a black bordered orange upperside with fine black marks crossed over the post median. Males have black knobs on antennae. There is a dark marginal area to the hindwing underside with a light crescent.

Swamp Verbena (*Verbena hastata*)
Robert H. Mohlenbrock @ USDA-NRCS PLANTS Database / USDA SCS. 1989. Midwest wetland flora: Field office illustrated guide to plant species. Midwest National Technical Center, Lincoln.

Swamp Verbena (*Verbena hastata*)

Also Known As: Blue Verbena, Blue Vervain, Simpler's Joy

Plant Description: With a height between 2 and 5 feet tall, this perennial has flower spikes that look like a pencil. Flowers are blue-purple and bloom between June and September. The flowers are branched in a form that looks like a candelabra. Stems are stout and square.

Growing Guide: Able to grow in any lighting, the swamp verbena prefers a wet or moist soil. Propagate by seed that have had a month of cool-moist stratification.

Interesting Facts: This plant has been used for depression, coughs, fevers, and jaundice. It has also been an herbal remedy for acne and skin wounds.

Warnings: This can interfere with hormone therapy and with blood pressure medication and should not be used without a doctor's recommendation. High doses of swamp verbena can cause vomiting and diarrhea.

Southern Distribution: Alabama, Arkansas, Georgia, Kentucky, Mississippi, North Carolina, Louisiana, South Carolina, Tennessee, Texas, Virginia, and West Virginia.

Classification: Family *Verbenaceae* – Verbena family

Genus *Verbena* L. – vervain

Species *Verbena hastata* L. – swamp verbena

Butterflies and Moths Attracted: It is a larval host to the Common Buckeye (*Junonia coenia*) butterfly. The common buckeye butterfly has a G5, or secure, NatureServe Global Status and a wingspan of 1 5/8-inches to 2 3/4-inches. It is brown with two eyespots and two orange cell bars on the forewing and two eyespots in the hindwing. It has a brown or tan hindwing underside in the summer and rose-red in the fall.

Narrowleaf Vervain (*Verbena simplex*)

Plant Description: This native grows up to 2 1/2 feet high with opposite narrow leaves. There are flower racemes at the end of the stems, lavender or white. Bloom season around two months long.

Growing Guide: Plant in full sun with a dry soil. Propagate by seed.

Southern Distribution: Alabama, Arkansas, Florida, Georgia, Kentucky, Mississippi, North Carolina, South Carolina, Tennessee, Texas, Virginia, and West Virginia.

Classification: Family *Verbenaceae* – Verbena family

Genus *Verbena* L. – vervain

Species *Verbena simplex* Lehm. – narrowleaf vervain

Butterflies and Moths Attracted: It is a larval host to the Common Buckeye (*Junonia coenia*) butterfly. The common buckeye butterfly has a G5, or secure, NatureServe Global Status and a wingspan of 1 5/8-inches to 2 3/4-inches. It is brown with two eyespots and two orange cell bars on the forewing and two eyespots in the hindwing. It has a brown or tan hindwing underside in the summer and rose-red in the fall.

Birdfoot Violet (*Viola pedata*)
Larry Allain @ USDA-NRCS PLANTS Database

Birdfoot Violet (*Viola pedata*)

Plant Description: Growing only 4 to 10 inches tall, this perennial has deeply cut leaves. Flowers are purple, from pale to dark in variance, and pansy-sized. Bloom season is between March and June. These flowers have orange anthers and dark streaks on the lowest petals.

Growing Guide: This violet needs partial shade or full shade and a dry acidic soil. Propagate by root cuttings or by seed. Seed will need 10 days of cold-moist stratification.

Interesting Facts: Unlike most violets, this particular one does not reproduce vegetatively.

Warnings: The plant is prone to crown rot in poorly draining soil.

Southern Distribution: Alabama, Arkansas, Georgia, Kentucky, Louisiana, Mississippi, North Carolina, South Carolina, Tennessee, Texas, Virginia, and West Virginia.

Classification: Family *Violaceae* – Violet family

Genus *Viola* L. – violet

Species *Viola pedata* L. – birdfoot violet

Butterflies and Moths Attracted: It is a larval host to the Regal Fritillary (*Speyeria idalia*) and the Variegated Fritillary (*Euptoieta claudia*) butterfly. With a G3, or vulnerable, NatureServe Global Status, the regal fritillary has a wingspan of 2 5/8-inches to 4 1/8-inches. A red-orange with black markings forewing upperside marks this large butterfly. The hindwing has a black background with white spots.

The variegated fritillary is secure with a G5 NatureServe Global Status and has a wingspan of 1 3/4-inches to 3 1/8-inches. Black spotted margins adorn an orange-brown wing with dark veins. There is a slight scallop to the hindwing and the underside is mottled.

Variegated Fritillary
(C) Mark Dreiling of Santee, CA

American Wisteria (*Wisteria frutescens*)
Robert H. Mohlenbrock @ USDA-NRCS PLANTS Database / USDA SCS. 1991. Southern wetland flora: Field office guide to plant species. South National Technical Center, Fort Worth.

American Wisteria (*Wisteria frutescens*)

Also Known As: Texas Wisteria, Kentucky Wisteria

Plant Description: This perennial grows 25 to 30 feet long with dark green deciduous leaves and clusters of flowers. Flowers can be white, blue, purple, pink or violet. Leaves are compound and shiny. Flowers are fragrant and come between May and June. It has bean-like brown pods that have its seeds.

Growing Guide: This wisteria should be planted in any lighting with a moist acidic or nearly neutral pH soil. It has a medium drought tolerance. Propagate by softwood cuttings or by seed. If grown from seed, it will be a few years before it will bloom.

Interesting Facts: This perennial will only bloom on new growth.

Warnings: Alkaline soil will make this plant chlorotic.

Southern Distribution: Alabama, Arkansas, Florida, Georgia, Kentucky, Louisiana, Mississippi, North Carolina, South Carolina, Tennessee, Texas, Virginia, and West Virginia.

Classification: Family *Fabaceae* – Pea family

Genus *Wisteria* Nutt. – wisteria

Species *Wisteria frutescens* (L.) Poir. – American wisteria

Butterflies and Moths Attracted: It is a larval host to the Marine Blue (*Leptotes marina*) in the states of Louisiana, Georgia, Mississippi, Tennessee, and Arkansas. It is also a larval host to the Long-tailed Skipper (*Urbanus proteus*), the Silver-spotted Skipper (*Epargyreus clarus*), and the Zarucco Duskywing (*Erynnis zarucco*) butterflies. The marine blue is secure with a NatureServe Global Status rank of G5. It has a wingspan between 7/8-inch and 1 1/8-inches. There is no white on the females but there is purple on the males; on both sexes the upperside is blue. The forewing's underside has a pale brown band.

The long-tailed skipper has a secure G5 NatureServe Global Status and a wingspan between 1 3/4-inches and 2 5/16-inches. With a dark black-brown body and long tails, this butterfly has blue-green wing bases and body. There is a dark band on the hindwing underside.

With a secure NatureServe Global Status rating of G5, the silver-spotted skipper butterfly isn't near extinction. It has a wingspan of 1 3/4-inches to 2 5/8-inches. There are forewing gold spots and a hindwing with a silver band on this black or brown-winged butterfly. The hindwing of a silver-spotted skipper will be lobed.

The Zarucco duskywing has a secure G5 NatureServe Global Status rating and a wingspan between 1 5/8-inches and 1 7/8-inches. It has a triangular hindwing that usually has brown fringes. There is a narrow pointed forewing and a dark brown upperside that has a reddish patch toward the forewing cell end.

Golden Zizia (*Zizia aurea*)
Larry Allain @ USDA-NRCS PLANTS Database

Golden Zizia (*Zizia aurea*)

Also Known As: Golden Alexanders

Plant Description: With erect stems and a branching form, this perennial grows 1 to 3 feet high. Stems have a red tone. Leaves are divided only once on the upper part of the plant while the lower leaves are divided three times. Flowers are yellow, appearing between April and August. They are in clusters and each bloom contains five sepals, petals, and stamens. Seed heads are purple in the summer when dry.

Growing Guide: The golden zizia prefers full sun or partial shade and a moist soil. Propagate by seed or division. Seed will need stratification and a cool soil to germinate.

Interesting Facts: The meadow parsnip (*Thaspium trifoliatum*) is also known as golden Alexanders.

Warnings: This is a short-lived plant.

Southern Distribution: Alabama, Arkansas, Florida, Georgia, Kentucky, Louisiana, Mississippi, North Carolina, South Carolina, Tennessee, Texas, Virginia, and West Virginia.

Classification: Family *Apiaceae* – Carrot family

Genus *Zizia* W.D.J. Koch – zizia

Species *Zizia aurea* (L.) W.D.J. Koch – golden zizia

Butterflies and Moths Attracted: It is a larval host to the Black Swallowtail (*Papilio polyxenes*) butterfly. The black swallowtail has a secure G5 NatureServe Global Status and a wingspan of 3 1/4-inches to 4 1/4-inches. With near black uppersides there is an orange spot with an internal black spot on the hindwing's inner edge. Females have a blue band on the hindwing and a row of yellow spots. Males have a band that is yellow near the wing's edge.

Black Swallowtail
(C) Mark Dreiling of Santee, CA

Chapter Four: Ornamental Grasses

Native ornamental grasses are not as well known or popular as grasses that originated in places like Eurasia. The imported grasses have an imposing or colorful appearance, though they do not offer the same type of rustic charm that native ornamental grasses contribute to the view in your garden.

Local grasses are hardy to the area in which they are native to. This means that they are able to tolerate the heat, humidity, rainfall, or lack of water in the native area. This is important when planning a butterfly garden - you will need plants that offer food and shelter to butterflies. Ornamental grasses may also help your garden retain water. The shade from taller varieties can reduce the amount of water evaporated by the sun and cool nearby plants.

Certain butterfly larvae will eat only certain types of plants and nothing else. By planting native grasses you expand the possibility that butterflies will be able to reproduce in your garden. Who knows, your garden may be the only area within miles that certain butterflies can lay their eggs!

When choosing native ornamental grasses and other plants for your butterfly garden, you will need to know which adult butterflies live near your home. You can check local agriculture extension websites or call their office for information on local butterfly population. They may be able to tell you which plants the larvae feed on. A simple Internet search can also point you in the right direction for the native grasses best for your garden.

Big Bluestem (*Andropogon gerardii*)
Jennifer Anderson @ USDA-NRCS PLANTS Database

Big Bluestem (*Andropogon gerardii*)

Also Known As: Turkeyfoot, *Andropogon gerardii var. chrysocomus*

Plant Description: Big bluestem grows 4 to 8 feet tall with blue-green stems. It is a bunchgrass that has a three-part seedhead that looks like the foot of a turkey. It has a maroon-tan color in the fall.

Growing Guide: It prefers full sun or partial shade with a moist soil. It has a high drought tolerance. Propagate by seeds or root division. Seed can use dry stratification and cold-moist stratification to help in germination.

Interesting Facts: This ornamental grass gives cover to over 24 species of songbirds.

Warnings: It can get aggressive.

Southern Distribution: Alabama, Arkansas, Florida, Georgia, Kentucky, Louisiana, Mississippi, North Carolina, South Carolina, Tennessee, Texas, Virginia, and West Virginia.

Classification: Family *Poaceae* – Grass family

Genus *Andropogon* L. – bluestem

Species *Andropogon gerardii* Vitman – big bluestem

Butterflies and Moths Attracted: It is a larval host to the Delaware Skipper (*Anatrytone logan*) and the Dusted Skipper (*Atrytonopsis hianna*). The Delaware skipper has a NatureServe Global Status of G5, or secure, and a wingspan between 1-inch and 1 11/16-inches. Yellow-orange wings have black veins and borders and a black bar on the forewing at the end of the cell. Underside can have dark orange veins. Males have paler markings and borders that are less wide than females.

The dusted skipper has a G4, or apparently secure, NatureServe Global Status rating and a wingspan of 1 1/4-inches to 1 11/16-inches. These butterflies have a gray-black upperside with white-spotted brown fringes. There is a gray underside to the hindwing and at least a single white dot at the base of the wings.

Delaware Skipper
(C) Mark Dreiling of Santee, CA

Broomsedge Bluestem (*Andropogon virginicus*)
Robert H. Mohlenbrock @ USDA-NRCS PLANTS Database / USDA SCS. 1991. Southern wetland flora: Field office guide to plant species. South National Technical Center, Fort Worth.

Broomsedge Bluestem (*Andropogon virginicus*)

Also Known As: Broom-sedge

Plant Description: Growing 2 to 5 feet high, the stems have seeds evenly distributed. The expanded racemes have fine hairs. This grass is green and clump forming, turning brown in the fall.

Growing Guide: Plant a broomsedge bluestem in partial shade and with moist soil. Propagate by root division or by seed.

Interesting Facts: Provides a grazing source for deer and a cover for birds.

Warnings: In can be aggressive and invade on disturbed lands.

Southern Distribution: Alabama, Arkansas, Florida, Georgia, Kentucky, Louisiana, Mississippi, North Carolina, South Carolina, Tennessee, Texas, Virginia, and West Virginia.

Classification: Family *Poaceae* – Grass family

Genus *Andropogon* L. – bluestem

Species *Andropogon virginicus* L. – broomsedge bluestem

Butterflies and Moths Attracted: It is a larval host to the Zabulon Skipper (*Poanes zabulon*). The Zabulon skipper has a NatureServe Global Status of G5, or secure, and a wingspan between 1 3/8-inches and 1 5/8-inches. Females have a purple-brown color with yellow spots on the upperside while the underside is brown, purple-gray, and has a white edge on the margin. Males have black borders and an underside of yellow with a dark brown base to the wings and outer margins.

Sideoats Grama (*Bouteloua curtipendula*)

Plant Description: Growing 2 to 3 feet tall, it is a clump-forming perennial grass. It has red or purple basal foliage and purple-tinted spikelets that look like oats. The grass turns tan in the fall. There are fibrous roots.

Growing Guide: Sideoats grama should be planted in full sun or partial shade in moist or dry well-drained soil. It is cold, drought, and heat tolerant. Propagate by seeds and by root division. Seed should be untreated if sown in the fall or sow in the spring after stratification. Divide in the spring or the fall so that the plant is dormant.

Interesting Facts: It is the state grass of Texas.

Southern Distribution: Alabama, Arkansas, Florida, Georgia, Kentucky, Louisiana, Mississippi, South Carolina, Tennessee, Texas, Virginia, and West Virginia.

Classification: Family *Poaceae* – Grass family

Genus *Bouteloua* Lag. – grama

Species *Bouteloua curtipendula* (Michx.) Torr. – sideoats grama

Butterflies and Moths Attracted: It is a food source for the Orange Skipperling (*Copaeodes aurantiaca*). In Texas, it is also a food source for Bronze Roadside Skipper (*Amblyscirtes aenus*). The orange skipperling has a G5, or secure, NatureServe Global Status and a wingspan between 3/4-inch and 1 1/8-inches. It is orange on both the top and bottom of the wings with the males having a black stigma below its forewing cell and the females having black edges on their forewing.

The bronze roadside skipper has a NatureServe Global Status of G4, or apparently secure, and a wingspan between 1-inch and 1 1/4-inches. A brown butterfly with a light orange hue, there are pale spots on the forewing and no markings on the hindwing. There is a red-brown hindwing underside with pale spots in a row.

Buffalograss (*Bouteloua dactyloides*)

Also Known As: *Buchloe dactyloides*

Plant Description: This particular grass has gray-green or blue-green foliage, growing three to 12 inches high. It has slender stems with curly leafblades and a tight seed head. It is generally long-lived.

Growing Guide: Plant buffalograss in full sun with a dry well-drained soil. Propagate by seed. Seed should have 1 1/2 months of cold moist stratification and needs light to germinate.

Interesting Facts: This makes for a food and nesting source for some mammals and birds.

Warnings: This will go dormant when its winter and in times of drought.

Southern Distribution: Arkansas, Georgia, Kentucky, Louisiana, Texas, and Virginia.

Classification: Family *Poaceae* – Grass family

Genus *Bouteloua* Lag. – grama

Species *Bouteloua dactyloides* (Nutt.) J.T. Columbus – buffalograss

Butterflies and Moths Attracted: It is a larval host to the Green Skipper (*Hesperia viridis*) in the states of Arkansas and Texas. Having a G4 NatureServe Global Status, or apparently secure rating, the green skipper has a wingspan between 1-inch and 1 1/2-inches. The bright gold-orange wings have a few pale-colored spots on the forewing, more on the females than males. There is a green-orange to yellow-orange hindwing with white spots. Males have a black male stigma on forewing.

Hairy Grama (*Bouteloua hirsuta*)

Plant Description: This perennial grass grows 10 to 18 inches tall. Stems are erect and leafy, with dense clumps. Seeds are on a curved seedhead and are oat-like in appearance. This grass has flowers but they are generally not seen.

Growing Guide: Plant this in partial shade with dry soil. It can be propagated by seed.

Interesting Facts: It normally is not found in pure strands.

Southern Distribution: Arkansas, Florida, Georgia, Louisiana, Mississippi, South Carolina, and Texas.

Classification: Family *Poaceae* – Grass family

Genus *Bouteloua* Lag. – grama

Species *Bouteloua hirsuta* Lag. – hairy grama

Butterflies and Moths Attracted: It is a larval host to the Green Skipper (*Hesperia viridis*) in the states of Arkansas and Texas. Having a G4 NatureServe Global Status, or apparently secure rating, the green skipper has a wingspan between 1-inch and 1 1/2-inches. The bright gold-orange wings have a few pale-colored spots on the forewing, more on the females than males. There is a green-orange to yellow-orange hindwing with white spots. Males have a black male stigma on forewing.

Inland Sea Oats (*Chasmanthium latifolium*) Larry Allain @ USDA-NRCS PLANTS Database

Inland Sea Oats (*Chasmanthium latifolium*)

Also Known As: Indian Wood Oats, River Oats, Upland Oats, *Uniola latifolia*, Flathead Oats, Upland Sea Oats

Plant Description: This perennial grows two to four feet tall with large dropping spikelets that have oat-like flowers. Leaves are like bamboo and blue-green in color, turning yellow-gold in the fall. Seeds will be ivory and then brown before dropping off.

Growing Guide: Plant inland sea oats in partial shade or full shade with a moist acidic soil. Soils that drain poorly are ok. Propagate by seed or root division. It can self-seed.

Interesting Facts: The seed stalks can be used in many types of floral arrangements.

Warnings: Can expand its boundaries rather aggressively due to the self-seeding.

Southern Distribution: Alabama, Arkansas, Florida, Georgia, Kentucky, Mississippi, Louisiana, North Carolina, South Carolina, Tennessee, Texas, Virginia, and West Virginia.

Classification: Family *Poaceae* – Grass family

Genus *Chasmanthium* Link – woodoats

Species *Chasmanthium latifolium* (Michx.) Yates – Indian woodoats

Butterflies and Moths Attracted: It is a larval host to the Pepper and Salt Skipper (*Amblyscirtes hegon*) and Bells Roadside Skipper (*Amblyscirtes belli*). In Texas, it is a larval host to the Bronze Roadside Skipper (*Amblyscirtes aenus*). The pepper and salt skipper is secure with a NatureServe Global Status of G5 and has a wingspan of 1-inch to 1 3/16-inches. There is a red-brown upperside to the wings and pale spots. Hindwing undersides have a pale band on gray-green coloring. Males have a black stigma on forewing.

The bells roadside skipper has a G4, or apparently secure, NatureServe Global Status and a wingspan between 1 3/16-inches and 1 1/4-inches. They have checkered fringes and a dark brown upperside. Underside of the wings has two rows of gray spots on a gray-black background. There are pale spots on the forewing.

The bronze roadside skipper has a NatureServe Global Status of G4, or apparently secure, and a wingspan between 1-inch and 1 1/4-inches. A brown butterfly with a light orange hue, there are pale spots on the forewing and no markings on the hindwing. There is a red-brown hindwing underside with pale spots in a row.

Bells Roadside Skipper
(C) Mark Dreiling of Santee, CA

Saltgrass (*Distichlis spicata*)
Sheri Hagwood @ USDA-NRCS PLANTS Database

Saltgrass (*Distichlis spicata*)

Also Known As: Coastal Salt Grass, Inland Salt-grass, *Distichlis stricta, Distichlis spicata var. stricta*

Plant Description: This warm-season grass grows up to 3 feet tall in an erect form. There are smooth spikelets for a seed head. A perennial, expect yellow grain between April and October.

Growing Guide: Saltgrass prefers full sun and a wet soil. It does fine in saline soils. Propagate by seed.

Southern Distribution: Alabama, Florida, Georgia, Louisiana, Mississippi, North Carolina, South Carolina, Texas, and Virginia

Classification: Family *Poaceae* – Grass family

Genus *Distichlis* Raf. – saltgrass

Species *Distichlis spicata* (L.) Greene – saltgrass

Butterflies and Moths Attracted: It is a larval host to the Salt Marsh Skipper (*Panoquina panoquin*). The salt marsh skipper has a NatureServe Global Status rating of G5, or secure, and a wingspan between 1 3/16-inches to 1 1/2-inches. There are dark brown wings and pointed forewings with the forewing upperside having pale spots. The hindwing underside has a white bark at the end of the cell and yellow veins.

Canada Wildrye (*Elymus canadensis*)
Larry Allain @ USDA-NRCS PLANTS Database

Canada Wildrye (*Elymus canadensis*)

Also Known As: Prairie Wildrye, Nodding Wildrye

Plant Description: Canada wildrye is a cool-season grass that is a perennial; however, it is short-lived. It grows 2 to 4 feet tall in an erect or arching growth pattern. Seed heads are oat-like and on spike-like terminals. It is easy to grow and has virtually no maintenance.

Growing Guide: Plant in full sun or partial shade with a moist well-drained soil. It can tolerate acidic soils and calcareous sand soils. Propagate by seed or root division. Seed may need 2 weeks of cold moist stratification. Seed needs not to be buried deep as it needs sun to germinate.

Interesting Facts: Seeds were used as a food source by some Native Americans. Today it is good for cattle grazing and for use in some dried floral arrangements.

Southern Distribution: Arkansas, Kentucky, North Carolina, Tennessee, Texas, Virginia, and West Virginia.

Classification: Family *Poaceae* – Grass family

Genus *Elymus* L. – wildrye

Species *Elymus canadensis* L. – Canada wildrye

Butterflies and Moths Attracted: It is a larval host to the Zabulon Skipper (*Poanes zabulon*). The Zabulon skipper has a NatureServe Global Status of G5, or secure, and a wingspan between 1 3/8-inches and 1 5/8-inches. Females have a purple-brown color with yellow spots on the upperside while the underside is brown, purple-gray, and has a white edge on the margin. Males have black borders and an underside of yellow with a dark brown base to the wings and outer margins.

Rice Cut Grass (*Leersia oryzoides*)

Plant Description: Growing from 2 1/2 to 5 feet high, this grass has prickly dark green leaves and greenish flower clusters. Flowers stay next to the dropping branches. It will be in bloom between June and October.

Growing Guide: Rice cut grass should be planted in partial shade with wet soil. It can grow well in standing water.

Warnings: It is considered a weed and its leaves can injure bare legs with its sharp edges.

Southern Distribution: Alabama, Arkansas, Florida, Georgia, Kentucky, Louisiana, Mississippi, North Carolina, South Carolina, Tennessee, Texas, Virginia, and West Virginia.

Classification: Family *Poaceae* – Grass family

Genus *Leersia* Sw. – cutgrass

Species *Leersia oryzoides* (L.) Sw. – rice cut grass

Butterflies and Moths Attracted: It is a food source for the Least Skipper (*Ancyloxypha numitor*). The least skipper butterfly is secure with a NatureServe Global Status of G5 and has a wingspan between 7/8-inch and 1 1/8-inches. There is an outer margin black border on the upperside of the forewing on an orange background. There is a black margin on the hindwing on a yellow-orange background. A black forewing underside is adorned with orange borders on tip and edge.

Least Skipper
(C) Mark Dreiling of Santee, CA

Switchgrass (*Panicum virgatum*)
Robert H. Mohlenbrock @ USDA-NRCS PLANTS Database / USDA SCS. 1991. Southern wetland flora: Field office guide to plant species. South National Technical Center, Fort Worth.

Switchgrass (*Panicum virgatum*)

Also Known As: Wand Panic Grass

Plant Description: This grass grows 3 to 6 feet tall in a clump formation. It has red-purple seed heads and bright green leaves that mature to yellow in the fall. It is a perennial with curly leaves and open lacy seed sprays between August and November.

Growing Guide: Plant switchgrass in full sun or partial shade in dry soils. Propagate by seed. Seed should be fresh if sown in fall or have been treated with dry stratification if sown in fall. Sow 1/4 inch deep.

Southern Distribution: Alabama, Arkansas, Florida, Georgia, Kentucky, Louisiana, North Carolina, South Carolina, Tennessee, Texas, Virginia, and West Virginia.

Classification: Family *Poaceae* – Grass family

Genus *Panicum* L. – panicgrass

Species *Panicum virgatum* L. – switchgrass

Butterflies and Moths Attracted: It is a food source for the Delaware Skipper (*Anatrytone logan*) and a larval host for the Dotted Skipper (*Hesperia attalus*). The Delaware skipper has a NatureServe Global Status of G5, or secure, and a wingspan between 1-inch and 1 11/16-inches. Yellow-orange wings have black veins and borders and a black bar on the forewing at the end of the cell. Underside can have dark orange veins. Males have paler markings and borders that are less wide than females.

The dotted skipper has a G3, or vulnerable, NatureServe Global Status and a wingspan between 1 3/8-inches and 1 5/8-inches. Upperside is brown, with pale spots on female and a brown-orange in the males with a dark border. Underside is a green-brown or dull orange. It is a variable-colored butterfly.

Little Bluestem (*Schizachyrium scoparium*)
L. Glasscock @ USDA-NRCS PLANTS Database / USDA SCS. 1991. Southern wetland flora: Field office guide to plant species. South National Technical Center, Fort Worth.

Little Bluestem (*Schizachyrium scoparium*)

Also Known As: *Schizachyrium scoparium var. scoparium, Andropogon scoparius*

Plant Description: With a fine-textured foliage, little bluestem has blue-green summer leaves and golden leaves in winter. It will grow between 1 1/2 to 3 feet tall. Stems are slender and can be mahogany-red with white seed tufts in the fall after a bluish color all spring.

Growing Guide: Plant in full sun or partial shade with a dry well-drained soil. It has a high drought tolerance. Propagate by root division or by seed that has been treated with dry stratification.

Warnings: It is intolerant of wetland locations.

Southern Distribution: Alabama, Arkansas, Florida, Georgia, Kentucky, Louisiana, Mississippi, North Carolina, South Carolina, Tennessee, Texas, Virginia, and West Virginia.

Classification: Family *Poaceae* – Grass family

Genus *Schizachyrium* Nees – little bluestem

Species *Schizachyrium scoparium* (Michx.) Nash – little bluestem

Butterflies and Moths Attracted: It is a larval host to the Dusted Skipper (*Atrytonopsis hianna*) and the Crossline Skipper (*Polites origenes*). It is also a larval host to the Indian Skipper (*Hesperia sassacus*) in the states of Alabama, Tennessee, Kentucky, Georgia, Virginia, West Virginia, and the Carolinas. It is also a larval host to the Ottoe Skipper (*Hesperia ottoe*) in a section of Arkansas. The dusted skipper has a G4, or apparently secure, NatureServe Global Status rating and a wingspan of 1 1/4-inches to 1 11/16-inches. These butterflies have a gray-black upperside with white-spotted brown fringes. There is a gray underside to the hindwing and at least a single white dot at the base of the wings.

The crossline skipper has a G5, or secure, NatureServe Global Status and a wingspan between 1 1/8-inches to 1 1/2-inches. It is dark brown and has orange markings on the upperside with a hindwing underside that is orange-brown with a band of spots. Females typically do not have orange on the forewing costa while the male has a long forewing stigma.

The ottoe skipper has a NatureServe Global Status of G3, or vulnerable, and a wingspan between 1 1/4-inches and 1 11/16-inches. With brown-orange wings on the upperside, males will have black outer margin edging and females have diffused borders and brighter coloring. There is a black or gray stigma on male forewing. Hindwings are yellow-orange on the underside.

The Indian skipper has a NatureServe Global Status of G5, or secure, and a wingspan between 1 1/4-inches to 1 3/8-inches. It has black markings on a yellow-orange background to its upperside and is yellow-orange with yellow spots in a band on the hindwing underside. The hindwings black border typically is toothed.

Woolgrass (*Scirpus cyperinus*)
Robert H. Mohlenbrock @ USDA-NRCS PLANTS Database / USDA SCS. 1989. Midwest wetland flora: Field office illustrated guide to plant species. Midwest National Technical Center, Lincoln.

Woolgrass (*Scirpus cyperinus*)

Also Known As: Marsh Bulrush, Cottongrass Bulrush, Teddybear Paws

Plant Description: A clump forming perennial, this grass grows three to six feet high. Brown bristles form around the nutlets making the plant appear fuzzy. It has an erect leafy stem.

Growing Guide: Woolgrass prefers full sun and a wet soil, either acidic or nearly neutral in pH. It does fine in standing water. Propagate by root division.

Interesting Facts: This grass is a cover for nesting birds; its seeds and roots eaten by waterfowl.

Southern Distribution: Alabama, Arkansas, Florida, Georgia, Kentucky, Louisiana, Mississippi, North Carolina, South Carolina, Tennessee, Texas, Virginia, and West Virginia.

Classification: Family *Cyperaceae* – Sedge family

Genus *Scirpus* L. – bulrush

Species *Scirpus cyperinus* (L.) Kunth – woolgrass

Butterflies and Moths Attracted: It is a larval host to the Dion Skipper (*Euphyes dion*). The Dion skipper has a G4, or apparently secure, NatureServe Global Status ranking and a wingspan that is between 1 7/16-inches to 1 3/4-inches. The upperside forewing is dark brown with females having orange spots and makes having a black stigma and an orange central area. There is a wide orange streak on the dark brown hindwing. There is a red-brown or orange-brown underside to the hindwing and two yellow-orange streaks.

Indiangrass (*Sorghastrum nutans*)
Robert H. Mohlenbrock @ USDA-NRCS PLANTS Database / USDA SCS. 1991. Southern wetland flora: Field office guide to plant species. South National Technical Center, Fort Worth.

Indiangrass (*Sorghastrum nutans*)

Also Known As: Yellow Indian Grass, *Sorghastrum avenaceum*

Plant Description: Indiangrass grows 3 to 8 feet tall in a bunch form. There are bright yellow flowers between August and October as well as blue-gray leaves. In fall, it will have a deep orange or a purple color. Seed heads are soft, large, and like plumes.

Growing Guide: It is very adaptable and able to grow in any lighting and moist to dry soil. It is drought tolerant. Propagate by seeds. Seed should be sown in the fall if untreated or in the spring after stratification. The root system is tangled and makes for difficult division.

Interesting Facts: It does well as a small mammal browse and as a nesting site for quail and pheasants.

Warnings: It should not be planted with fragile wildflowers as it can be aggressive.

Southern Distribution: Alabama, Arkansas, Florida, Georgia, Kentucky, Louisiana, Mississippi, North Carolina, South Carolina, Tennessee, Texas, Virginia, and West Virginia.

Classification: Family *Poaceae* – Grass family

Genus *Sorghastrum* Nash – Indiangrass

Species *Sorghastrum nutans* (L.) Nash – Indiangrass

Butterflies and Moths Attracted: It is a food source for the Pepper and Salt Skipper (*Amblyscirtes hegon*). The pepper and salt skipper is secure with a NatureServe Global Status of G5 and has a wingspan of 1-inch to 1 3/16-inches. There is a red-brown upperside to the wings and pale spots. Hindwing undersides have a pale band on gray-green coloring. Males have a black stigma on forewing.

Saltmarsh Cordgrass (*Spartina alterniflora*)
USDA-NRCS PLANTS Database

Saltmarsh Cordgrass (*Spartina alterniflora*)

Also Known As: Salt Cordgrass, Smooth Cordgrass

Plant Description: This grass grows 3 to 8 feet tall with green foliage that has a silver-white underside. Blooms are on 4 to 12 inch spikes and bloom between the end of summer and the fall season. Seed will follow the end of the blooming season.

Growing Guide: Grow saltmarsh cordgrass in full sun with wet soil. Soil can be alkaline to acidic and it adapts. It has a very low drought tolerance. Propagate by root division.

Interesting Facts: Roots, seeds, and leaves are used as food for waterfowl, deer, and muskrats.

Southern Distribution: Alabama, Florida, Georgia, Louisiana, Mississippi, North Carolina, South Carolina, Texas, and Virginia.

Classification: Family *Poaceae* – Grass family

Genus *Spartina* Schreb. – cordgrass

Species *Spartina alterniflora* Loisel. – smooth cordgrass

Butterflies and Moths Attracted: It is a larval host to the Louisiana-eyed Silkmoth (*Automeris louisiana*). The Louisiana-eyed silkmoth has a GU, or undetermined, NatureServe Global Status and a wingspan between 2 1/2-inches and 3 1/2-inches. There are yellow or light brown margins to the brown or light-yellow brown wings. There is some pink on the inner margins of the yellow-brown or orange hindwing. The hindwings will also have a white dash and black and blue eyespots.

Purpletop Tridens (*Tridens flavus*)
Larry Allain @ USDA-NRCS PLANTS Database

Purpletop Tridens (*Tridens flavus*)

Also Known As: Redtop Tridens, Purpletop, Redtop, Tall Redtop, Tall Redtop Tridens

Plant Description: Growing 2 1/2 to 7 feet high, this native perennial has red-purple spikelets and wide spaced drooping branches. The grass turns brown in the fall season.

Growing Guide: Purpletop tridens needs partial shade and a dry soil. It can be propagated by seed or by division.

Interesting Facts: This grass makes a good grazing grass for livestock.

Southern Distribution: Alabama, Arkansas, Florida, Georgia, Kentucky, Louisiana, Mississippi, North Carolina, South Carolina, Tennessee, Texas, Virginia, and West Virginia.

Classification: Family *Poaceae* – Grass family

Genus *Tridens* Roem. & Schult. – tridens

Species *Tridens flavus* (L.) Hitchc. – purpletop tridens

Butterflies and Moths Attracted: It is a larval host to the Crossline Skipper (*Polites origenes*), Little Glassywing (*Pompeius verna*), Common Wood Nymph (*Cercyonis pegala*), and the Broad-winged Skipper (*Poanes viator*). The crossline skipper has a G5, or secure, NatureServe Global Status and a wingspan between 1 1/8-inches to 1 1/2-inches. It is dark brown and has orange markings on the upperside with a hindwing underside that is orange-brown with a band of spots. Females typically do not have orange on the forewing costa while the male has a long forewing stigma.

Little glassywing has a NatureServe Global Status of G5, or secure, and a wingspan between 1 1/16-inches and 1 1/2-inches. With black or black-brown wings, there is a transparent spot at the end of the forewing stigma in males and a square spot at the end of the cell in female's forewing. The black underside has a purple hue to it and some pale spots.

The common wood nymph has a G5, or secure, NatureServe Global Status and a wingspan between 1 3/4-inches and 3-inches. There is variable colorings on this butterfly but most are brown with yellow-ringed eyespots on the forewing upperside. There are eyespots on the hindwing as well.

Broad-winged skipper has a NatureServe Global Status ranking of G5, or secure, and a wingspan that is between 1 1/4-inches and 2 1/4-inches. The round forewing is dark brown on the upperside with yellow-orange areas and cream spots. The orange hindwing has black veins and borders and an underside of orange-brown with a yellow-orange streak. The underside also has yellow-orange spots that are squared.

Eastern Gamagrass (*Tripsacum dactyloides*)
Larry Allain @ USDA-NRCS PLANTS Database

Eastern Gamagrass (*Tripsacum dactyloides*)

Plant Description: This perennial grass grows up to 10 feet in height, but it is typically between 2 and 3 feet. It has purple stigmas and orange stamens. This grass has terminal inflorescences; bloom time between April and June.

Growing Guide: Plant Eastern gamagrass in partial shade and in moist soil. Propagate by seed or by clump division.

Interesting Facts: Deer love the seeds, as it is a relative of the corn plant.

Warnings: Edges of the leaf blades are very sharp and can injure.

Southern Distribution: Alabama, Arkansas, Florida, Georiga, Kentucky, Louisiana, Mississippi, North Carolina, South Carolina, Tennessee, Texas, Virginia, and West Virginia.

Classification: Family *Poaceae* – Grass family

Genus *Tripsacum* L. – gamagrass

Species *Tripsacum dactyloides* (L.) L. – eastern gamagrass

Butterflies and Moths Attracted: It is a larval host to the Byssus Skipper (*Problema byssus*). The Byssus skipper has a G3, or vulnerable, NatureServe Global Status rank and a wingspan between 1 7/16-inches and 1 13/16-inches. The upperside has at the end of the cell a black bar on a yellow-orange background with black borders. Females tend to be darker than the males and have a rust or orange hindwing underside compared to the yellow underside in males.

Chapter Five: Native Trees

Typical ornamental gardening practices of the past incorporated fast growing species of trees that were not native to North America; if the trees were native to the continent they may have been imported from areas that had different growing conditions. In some cases this led to an invasive species taking hold and crowding out the local trees. One example of this is the Black Locust - a fast growing tree with large, sharp pointed seed pods. These pods can be spread over a large area in just one season. When the infant trees grow, they take up valuable nutrients that native seedlings need.

Another example of this is the Asian Tree of Heaven, a very fast growing tree that creates a canopy in just one growing season. These trees are notoriously hard to remove as their roots will sends up shoots year after year. If allowed to grow, one tree can turn into ten and a canopy that smothers native species can be created in less than five years.

During the planning stage of an ornamental garden, consider using native species. The trees that grow in your area are suited for the growing conditions that may be unique to your locality. These trees also have a resistance to local diseases that may affect imported species. Think of native trees as having received an immunization from nature.

Planting native trees not only brings a local charm to your ornamental garden, it helps protect potentially endangered plants from becoming extinct. Plant extinction is a problem that is larger than the animal extinction issue, though most people are not aware of it. Sustaining a population of native trees helps local wildlife as human expansion is continuously crowding out plant species.

Pawpaw (*Asimina triloba*)
Larry Allain @ USDA-NRCS PLANTS Database

Pawpaw (*Asimina triloba*)

Also Known As: Indian Banana, *Annona triloba*

Plant Description: Asimina triloba grows 10 to 40 feet high; beginning with a rusty down covering that matures smooth. Leaves are bright green and turn yellow-green. Flowers are purple and fruits are yellow or dark-green.

Growing Guide: Grow a pawpaw in full sun or partial shade and moist soil. Propagate by root cuttings, layering, or by seed. Seed will need scarification and stratification.

Interesting Facts: First Nations and European settlers once used the fruits as a food source. Today, fruits are still used as a food source for small mammals.

Warnings: The fruit can cause stomach upset when eaten and contact dermatitis when handled. The leaves are also irritating to some individuals.

Southern Distribution: Alabama, Arkansas, Florida, Georgia, Kentucky, Louisiana, North Carolina, South Carolina, Tennessee, Texas, Virginia, and West Virginia.

Classification: Family *Annonaceae* – Custard-apple family

Genus *Asimina* Adans. – pawpaw

Species *Asimina triloba* (L.) Dunal – pawpaw

Butterflies and Moths Attracted: It is a larval host to the Zebra Swallowtail (*Eurytides marcellus*) butterfly and the Pawpaw Sphinx (*Dolba hyloeus*) moth. The zebra swallowtail has a G5, secure, NatureServe Global Status and a wingspan between 2 1/2-inches and 4-inches. There are black stripes on a white-green background, giving it a zebra look. There are long tails on hindwing. In spring, it will be smaller and lighter in color.

The pawpaw sphinx moth is secure with a G5 NatureServe Global Status and a wingspan between 2-inches and 2 11/16-inches. It is dark brown with white dust-like scales. There may be red or yellow-brown on the wings as well.

Cherry Birch (*Betula lenta*)

Also Known As: Sweet Birch

Plant Description: The cherry birch grows 50 to 75 feet tall with aromatic deciduous leaves. Bark is scaly and brown-black. Leaves and twigs smell like wintergreen when crushed. Foliage will turn gold-yellow in the fall. Flowers are in catkins, blooming between April and May.

Growing Guide: Plant a cherry birch in partial to full shade with a moist or dry, acidic, well-drained soil. Propagate by seed and do not plant them too deep into the ground. If the seeds cannot get light to germinate, they may need 30 days of cold stratification.

Interesting Facts: The oil, better known as oil of wintergreen, used to flavor drugs and candy. Today the oil is manufactured in other ways.

Warnings: It can be prone to many plant diseases.

Southern Distribution: Alabama, Georgia, Kentucky, Mississippi, North Carolina, South Carolina, Tennessee, Virginia, and West Virginia.

Classification: Family *Betulaceae* – Birch family

Genus *Betula* L. – birch

Species *Betula lenta* L. – sweet birch

Butterflies and Moths Attracted: It is a food source for the Green Comma (*Polygonia faunus*) in the states of Georgia, Tennessee, Kentucky, Alabama, the Carolinas, Virginia, and West Virginia. The green comma is secure with a G5 NatureServe Global Status and has a wingspan between 1 3/4-inches and 2 1/1-inches. It is a variable butterfly, but generally has ragged wing edges with dark borders on a red-brown upperside and a yellow spotted border on the hindwing. There is a brown underside with a paler outer half and greenish spots on the submargin. There is a silver spot in the center of the hindwing that is shaped like a "C" or an "L".

American Hornbeam (*Carpinus caroliniana*)

Also Known As: Musclewood, Ironwood, Blue Beech

Plant Description: Growing 35 to 50 feet high, this tree has long spreading branches and deciduous blue-green leaves. Leaves will turn a nice scarlet-orange in the fall season. Bark is pale gray and smooth with bulges. Fruits are paper-like and hang down.

Growing Guide: The American hornbeam prefers partial to full shade with a moist soil that is nearly neutral in pH. Propagate by seed that is planted right after collection or after two to three months of cold-moist stratification if planted in the spring.

Interesting Facts: The name is given because of the wood's hardness. It is used for handles and for levers.

Warnings: Leaves of the American hornbeam may be susceptible to black mold.

Southern Distribution: Alabama, Arkansas, Florida, Georgia, Kentucky, Louisiana, Mississippi, North Carolina, South Carolina, Tennessee, Texas, Virginia, and West Virginia.

Classification: Family *Betulaceae* – Birch family

Genus *Carpinus* L. – hornbeam

Species *Carpinus caroliniana* Walter – American hornbeam

Butterflies and Moths Attracted: It is a larval host to the Eastern Tiger Swallowtail (*Papilio glaucus*) and the Striped Hairstreak (*Satyrium liparops*). Secure with a NatureServe Global Status of G5, the Eastern tiger swallowtail has a wingspan between 3 5/8-inches and 6 1/2-inches. Male butterflies have dark tiger-striped yellow wings. Females, while they may be colored like that, can also be black with dark striped shadows. Female hindwings have blue iridescent scales and a marginal orange spot.

Females have a marginal spotted row on the underside of the forewing.

Secure with a G5 NatureServe Global Status, the striped hairstreak has a wingspan between 1-inch and 1 1/2-inches. There is a long and a short tail. There are dark brown wings with white stripes and an orange-topped blue tail spot.

Eastern Tiger Swallowtail
(C) Mark Dreiling of Santee, CA

Black Hickory (*Carya texana*)

Plant Description: Growing up to 40 feet high, this small perennial tree has compound leaves that are alternate on the twig. Buds are small and it will fruit as a nut. It blooms red in March.

Growing Guide: This hickory prefers partial shade and a dry well-drained area. Propagate either by seed sown as soon as collected or after stratification if sown in the spring. Other propagation methods include hardwood cuttings.

Interesting Facts: It is both a nesting site for birds and a food browse for deer.

Warnings: This has a large taproot and does not transplant easily.

Southern Distribution: Alabama, Arkansas, Georgia, Kentucky, Louisiana, Mississippi, Tennessee, and Texas

Classification: Family *Juglandaceae* – Walnut family

Genus *Carya* Nutt. – hickory

Species *Carya texana* Buckley – black hickory

Butterflies and Moths Attracted: It is a larval host to the Banded Hairstreak (*Satyrium calanus*). The banded hairstreak has a NatureServe Global Status of G5, secure, and a wingspan of one-inch to 1 1/2-inches wide. There is a short and a long tail on the brown hindwing. Underside is darker with dark colored dashes with white edges. There is a blue tail spot and some orange near the tailspot.

Sugar Hackberry (*Celtis laevigata*)
Larry Allain @ USDA-NRCS PLANTS Database

Sugar Hackberry (*Celtis laevigata*)

Also Known As: Sugarberry, Hackberry, Texas Sugarberry, Palo Blanco

Plant Description: This broad deciduous tree can grow up to 80 feet tall and wide. Branches grow in a spreading or drooping style with long leaves and smooth margins. It has orange-red to black fruits. Bark on the tree will be smooth and pale.

Growing Guide: This tree prefers partial shade and dry soil. Propagate by seed, suckers, root sprouts, or young wood. Seeds should be sown fresh after collection or be stratified by cold-moist stratification for two to three months if sowing in the spring.

Interesting Facts: The wood from the sugar hackberry is used for plywood, flooring, posts, furniture, and as a crating material. The fruit from it is eaten by ten species of birds such as the robin and mockingbird.

Warnings: This tree frequently becomes parasitized by mistletoe. It is prone to the wooly aphid and the Asian woolly hackberry aphid.

Southern Distribution: Alabama, Arkansas, Florida, Georgia, Kentucky, Louisiana, Mississippi, North Carolina, South Carolina, Tennessee, Texas, Virginia, and West Virginia.

Classification: Family *Ulmaceae* – Elm family

Genus *Celtis* L. – hackberry

Species *Celtis laevigata* Willd. – sugarberry

Butterflies and Moths Attracted: It is a larval host for the Hackberry Emperor (*Asterocampa celtis*), Tawny Emperor (*Asterocampa clyton*), American Snout (*Libytheana carinenta*), and Question Mark (*Polygonia interrogationis*) butterflies.

The hackberry emperor has a NatureServe Global Status of G5, or secure, and a wingspan of 1 3/8-inches to 2 1/2-inches. It is a variable butterfly with a red-brown upperside and an eyespot on forewing. There is a row of white spots on forewing. The cell has a black bar and two black spots on it.

With a G5 secure NatureServe Global Status, the tawny emperor butterfly has a wingspan between 1 5/8-inches and 2 3/4-inches. It is a variably-colored butterfly, but typically brown on its upperside with two brown bars in the forewing cells. Upperside to the hindwing is either all black or orange with submarginal black spots.

The American snout butterfly has a G5, or secure, NatureServe Global Status and a wingspan between 1 3/8-inches and 2-inches. With a brown upperside, there is a basal orange color to the forewing with the outer half having white spots. There is a violet-gray or mottled hindwing underside.

The question mark butterfly has a G5, or secure, NatureServe Global Status and a wingspan between 2 1/4-inches and 3-inches. It is red-orange with black spots and a hooked forewing. There is a light brown underside with a pearl-white question mark in center of the hindwing. Winter butterflies have a longer tail than summer butterflies and have a hindwing upperside that is more orange than the blacker summer form.

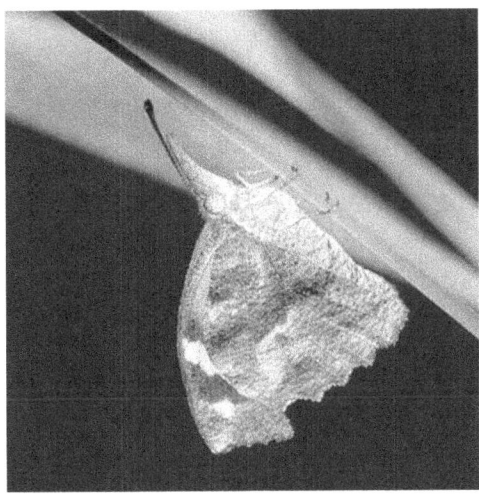

American Snout
(C) Mark Dreiling of Santee, CA

Common Hackberry (*Celtis occidentalis*)
USDA-NRCS PLANTS Database / Herman, D.E., et al. 1996. North Dakota tree handbook. USDA NRCS ND State Soil Conservation Committee; NDSU Extension and Western Area Power Administration, Bismarck.

Common Hackberry (*Celtis occidentalis*)

Plant Description: Growing 60 to 100 feet tall, the common hackberry has deciduous dull green leaves and clusters of berries. Berries are dark purple or orange-brown. It grows in an erratic form with spreading branches. Bark that has matured will have corky projections on it.

Growing Guide: It can be planted in any lighting or soil type as long as it has a nearly neutral pH. It has high drought tolerance. Propagate by fresh seed in fall or stratified seed in the spring. It may need two to three months of stratification. Other propagation methods include suckers and root cuttings.

Interesting Facts: It has been used as a Native American medicinal for colds and sore throats. The dried fruit was used by the Dakota people for a spice.

Warnings: Hackberries can be prone to mites, wooly aphids, Asian woolly hackberry aphid, and fungi. Its leaves can get jumping plant lice, which show up as rounded galls on the leaves.

Southern Distribution: Alabama, Arkansas, Florida, Georgia, Kentucky, Mississippi, North Carolina, South Carolina, Tennessee, Texas, Virginia, and West Virginia.

Classification: Family *Ulmaceae* – Elm family

Genus *Celtis* L. – hackberry

Species *Celtis occidentalis* L. – common hackberry

Butterflies and Moths Attracted: It is a food source for the Wild Cherry Sphinx moth (*Sphinx drupiferarum*) and a host plant for the Hackberry Emperor (*Asterocampa celtis*), Tawny Emperor (*Asterocampa clyton*), American Snout (*Libytheana carinenta*), and Question Mark (*Polygonia interrogationis*) butterflies. The wild cherry sphinx has a NatureServe Global Status of G5, or secure, and a wingspan between 3 1/4-inches and 4 5/16-inches. It is dark gray on the forewing upperside and dark gray on the hindwing. There is a single white band on the costa and the outer margin of the forewing and two white bands on the hindwing.

The hackberry emperor has a NatureServe Global Status of G5, or secure, and a wingspan of 1 3/8-inches to 2 1/2-inches. It is a variable butterfly with a red-brown upperside and an eyespot on forewing. There is a row of white spots on forewing. The cell has a black bar and two black spots on it.

With a G5 secure NatureServe Global Status, the tawny emperor butterfly has a wingspan between 1 5/8-inches and 2 3/4-inches. It is a variably-colored butterfly, but typically brown on its upperside with two brown bars in the forewing cells. Upperside to the hindwing is either all black or orange with submarginal black spots.

The American snout butterfly has a G5, or secure, NatureServe Global Status and a wingspan between 1 3/8-inches and 2-inches. With a brown upperside, there is a basal orange color to the forewing with the outer half having white spots. There is a violet-gray or mottled hindwing underside.

The question mark butterfly has a G5, or secure, NatureServe Global Status and a wingspan between 2 1/4-inches and 3-inches. It is red-orange with black spots and a hooked forewing. There is a light brown underside with a pearl-white question mark in center of the hindwing. Winter butterflies have a longer tail than summer butterflies and have a hindwing upperside that is more orange than the blacker summer form.

Question Mark
(C) Mark Dreiling of Santee, CA

Flowering Dogwood (*Cornus florida*)
Robert H. Mohlenbrock @ USDA-NRCS PLANTS Database / USDA NRCS. 1995. Northeast wetland flora: Field office guide to plant species. Northeast National Technical Center, Chester.

Flowering Dogwood (*Cornus florida*)

Also Known As: Virginia Dogwood

Plant Description: The flowering dogwood grows 20 to 40 feet tall in a spreading form. It can have a single or multiple trunks. Flowers are showy, white or pink, and long-lasting. Fruits are red as is the fall foliage on this tree. Flowers bloom between March and October.

Growing Guide: *Cornus florida* prefers partial to full shade conditions and acidic well-drained soil. Soil can be moist or dry. It is cold tolerant. Propagate by seed that is sown after collecting or, if sowing in the spring, after cold-moist stratification for one to two months.

Interesting Facts: The roots and bark have been used as a red or scarlet dye. Bark from the flowering dogwood has also been a folklore remedy for fevers, serving as a quinine substitute during the Civil War.

Warnings: It will need pruning to maintain shape.

Southern Distribution: Alabama, Arkansas, Florida, Georgia, Kentucky, Louisiana, Mississippi, North Carolina, South Carolina, Tennessee, Texas, Virginia, and West Virginia.

Classification: Family *Cornaceae* – Dogwood family

Genus *Cornus* L. – dogwood

Species *Cornus florida* L. – flowering dogwood

Butterflies and Moths Attracted: It is a larval host to the Spring Azure (*Celastrina ladon*). The spring azure has an apparent secure rating on NatureServe Global Status with a G4 rating. Its wingspan is between 7/8-inch and 1 3/8-inches. It has an upperside of a blue forewing and a gray-white underside.

Cockspur Hawthorn (*Crataegus crus-galli*)
Robert H. Mohlenbrock @ USDA-NRCS PLANTS Database / USDA SCS. 1991. Southern wetland flora: Field office guide to plant species. South National Technical Center, Fort Worth.

Cockspur Hawthorn (*Crataegus crus-galli*)

Plant Description: A small tree growing 20 to 35 feet high with a short trunk, it has glossy green leaves with orange or red fall color. Bark is exfoliating. Flowers are white and in clusters. Fruits are small red apples.

Growing Guide: Grow this hawthorn in any lighting and in any type of acidic well-drained soil. Propagate by seed that have had an acid-bath scarification and then four months of warm stratification.

Interesting Facts: The long spines on this tree have been once used as pins.

Warnings: This tree is prone to rust, insects, and fire blight. It also is a thorny tree.

Southern Distribution: Alabama, Arkansas, Florida, Georgia, Kentucky, Louisiana, Mississippi, North Carolina, South Carolina, Tennessee, Texas, Virginia, and West Virginia.

Classification: Family *Rosaceae* – Rose family

Genus *Crataegus* L. – hawthorn

Species *Crataegus crus-galli* L. – cockspur hawthorn

Butterflies and Moths Attracted: It is a larval host to the Banded Hairstreak (*Satyrium calanus*), Striped Hairstreak (*Satyrium liparops*), and the Gray Hairstreak (*Strymon melinus*). The banded hairstreak has a NatureServe Global Status of G5, secure, and a wingspan of one-inch to 1 1/2-inches wide. There is a short and a long tail on the brown hindwing. Underside is darker with dark colored dashes with white edges. There is a blue tail spot and some orange near the tailspot.

Secure with a G5 NatureServe Global Status, the striped hairstreak has a wingspan between 1-inch and 1 1/2-inches. There is a long and a short tail. There are dark brown wings with white stripes and an orange-topped blue tail spot.

The gray hairstreak has a secure rating, or G5, for its NatureServe Global Status and a wingspan between 7/8-inch and 1 3/8-inches. It is blue-gray with a red spot near the tail. There is one tail. The spring or fall variable of the butterfly is gray on the underside while the summer variable is pale gray. There is a white postmedian line that is bordered in orange.

Green Hawthorn (*Crataegus viridis*)
Robert H. Mohlenbrock @ USDA-NRCS PLANTS Database / USDA SCS. 1991. Southern wetland flora: Field office guide to plant species. South National Technical Center, Fort Worth.

Green Hawthorn (*Crataegus viridis*)

Also Known As: Southern Thorn

Plant Description: This member of the rose family grows 20 to 35 feet high and 20 to 35 feet wide. There is a dense crown of shiny yellow-green leaves. Fruits are bright red or orange. Flowers are white and showy, blooming between March and April.

Growing Guide: This grows well in partial shade and wet soils. Propagate by seed. Seed may need a two to three hour acid bath scarification if the endocarp is tough and then four months of warm stratification followed by four and a half months of cool stratification.

Southern Distribution: Alabama, Arkansas, Florida, Georgia, Kentucky, Louisiana, Mississippi, North Carolina, South Carolina, Tennessee, Texas, Virginia, and West Virginia.

Classification: Family *Rosaceae* – Rose family

Genus *Crataegus* L. – hawthorn

Species *Crataegus viridis* L. – green hawthorn

Butterflies and Moths Attracted: It is a larval host to the Banded Hairstreak (*Satyrium calanus*), the Gray Hairstreak (*Strymon melinus*), and the Red-banded Hairstreak (*Calycopis cecrops*). The banded hairstreak has a NatureServe Global Status of G5, secure, and a wingspan of one-inch to 1 1/2-inches wide. There is a short and a long tail on the brown hindwing. Underside is darker with dark colored dashes with white edges. There is a blue tail spot and some orange near the tailspot.

The gray hairstreak has a secure rating, or G5, for its NatureServe Global Status and a wingspan between 7/8-inch and 1 3/8-inches. It is blue-gray with a red spot near the tail. There is one tail. The spring or fall variable of the butterfly is gray on the underside while the summer variable is pale gray. There is a white postmedian line that is bordered in orange.

The red-banded hairstreak is secure with a G5 NatureServe Global Status and has a wingspan of 7/8-inch to 1 1/4-inches. The hindwing has two tails and is blue, with a brown forewing. The underside is gray-brown with a white line with red-orange borders.

American Beech (*Fagus grandifolia*)

Also Known As: *Fagus grandifolia var. caroliniana*

Plant Description: Growing 50 to 80 feet high on average with a maximum of 120 feet, this beech has smooth light gray bark. Foliage is simple, glossy, and dark green. In the fall it has a copper color.

Growing Guide: The American beech prefers partial to full shade and a moist well-drained soil. Propagate by seed that is sown fresh after collection in the fall or after three months of cold-moist stratification for spring sowing.

Interesting Facts: It is believed that the bark of the Beech tree was used to carve some of the earliest Sanskrit characters. It is a great source of wildlife food, especially squirrels, bears, game birds, and raccoons.

Warnings: This tree has a low toxicity for its raw nuts. It also is not drought tolerant and has a susceptibility to root zone disturbance.

Southern Distribution: Alabama, Arkansas, Florida, Georgia, Kentucky, Louisiana, Mississippi, North Carolina, South Carolina, Tennessee, Texas, Virginia, and West Virginia.

Classification: Family *Fagaceae* – Beech family

Genus *Fagus* L. – beech

Species *Fagus grandifolia* Ehrh. – American beech

Butterflies and Moths Attracted: It is a larval host to the Early Hairstreak (*Erora laeta*) in the upper south portions of Georgia, Tennessee, Virginia, and the Carolinas. The early hairstreak has a G4, or apparently secure, NatureServe Global Status and a wingspan between 7/8-inch and 15/16-inch. It is blue and black and there are no tails. Females are bluer than the males. The hindwing has two bands of orange dots and a turquoise underside.

White Ash (*Fraxinus americana*)
Robert H. Mohlenbrock @ USDA-NRCS PLANTS Database / USDA NRCS. 1995. Northeast wetland flora: Field office guide to plant species. Northeast National Technical Center, Chester.

White Ash (*Fraxinus americana*)

Plant Description: This is a large tree, growing 75 to 120 feet high, with a dense crown. Foliage is green and turns yellow before its fall season color of purple. The undersides to the leaves are paler.

Growing Guide: It grows fine in any lighting and soil moisture. Soils should be acidic. It is cold tolerant. Propagate by seed that have are freshly collected or after one to two months of stratification.

Interesting Facts: This was used to make a yellow dye in some Native American tribes. The leaf juice has been used as a folklore remedy for stings and bites.

Warnings: It is a species that can have problems with disease and pest damage.

Southern Distribution: Alabama, Arkansas, Florida, Georgia, Kentucky, Louisiana, Mississippi, North Carolina, South Carolina, Tennessee, Texas, Virginia, and West Virginia.

Classification: Family *Oleaceae* – Olive family

Genus *Fraxinus* L. – ash

Species *Fraxinus americana* L. – white ash

Butterflies and Moths Attracted: It is a larval host to the Eastern Tiger Swallowtail (*Papilio glaucus*), Hickory Hairstreak (*Satyrium caryaevorus*), Mourning Cloak (*Nymphalis antiopa*), and the Viceroy (*Limenitis archippus*). Secure with a NatureServe Global Status of G5, the Eastern tiger swallowtail has a wingspan between 3 5/8-inches and 6 1/2-inches. Male butterflies have dark tiger-striped yellow wings. Females, while they may be colored like that, can also be black with dark striped shadows. Female hindwings have blue iridescent scales and a marginal orange spot. Females have a marginal spotted row on the underside of the forewing.

With a G4, or apparently secure, NatureServe Global Status, the hickory hairstreak has a wingspan of 1 1/8-inches to 1 3/8-inches. It has a tail on the hindwing and is light brown with white dashes on an offset. There is a blue tail spot on hindwing and a black topped orange eyespot.

The mourning cloak butterfly has a secure ranking with a NatureServe Global status of G5, it also has a wingspan between 2 1/4-inches and 4-inches. There are irregular borders and short projections on the wings, with a purple-black upperside. There is a yellow border and blue spots on a row on the outer margin of the wings.

Secure with a NatureServe Global Status of G5, the viceroy has a wingspan of 2 1/2-inches to 3 3/8-inches. It mimics the monarch in coloring, with and orange and black upperside (rarely brown instead of orange, depending on location). The viceroy has hindwing black lines and white dots in a row on the black marginal band.

Viceroy
(C) Mark Dreiling of Santee, CA

Green Ash (*Fraxinus pennsylvanica*)
USDA-NRCS PLANTS Database / Herman, D.E., et al. 1996. North Dakota tree handbook. USDA NRCS ND State Soil
Conservation Committee; NDSU Extension and Western Area Power Administration, Bismarck.

Green Ash (*Fraxinus pennsylvanica*)

Also Known As: Red Ash, *Fraxinus pennsylvanica var. lanceolata*

Plant Description: This deciduous tree grows 50 to 75 feet high in an upright form. Leaves are divided and slightly toothed on the margins. Its deep green color turns to yellow in the fall. Flowers are clustered and small. Dry winged fruits are clustered and resemble a blade.

Growing Guide: This ash grows well in any lighting condition and in any type of soil moisture. Soils should be nearly neutral in pH. Propagate by pretreated seed that has had warm-moist stratification for two months and then four months of cool-moist stratification.

Interesting Facts: The bark of the green ash can make a red dye.

Southern Distribution: Alabama, Arkansas, Florida, Georgia, Kentucky, Louisiana, Mississippi, North Carolina, South Carolina, Tennessee, Texas, Virginia, and West Virginia.

Classification: Family *Oleaceae* – Olive family

Genus *Fraxinus* L. – ash

Species *Fraxinus pennsylvanica* Marsh. – green ash

Butterflies and Moths Attracted: It is a larval host to the Mourning Cloak (*Nymphalis antiopa*) and Eastern Tiger Swallowtail (*Papilio glaucus*). The mourning cloak butterfly has a secure ranking with a NatureServe Global status of G5, it also has a wingspan between 2 1/4-inches and 4-inches. There are irregular borders and short projections on the wings, with a purple-black upperside. There is a yellow border and blue spots on a row on the outer margin of the wings.

Secure with a NatureServe Global Status of G5, the Eastern tiger swallowtail has a wingspan between 3 5/8-inches and 6 1/2-inches. Male butterflies have dark tiger-striped yellow wings. Females, while they may be colored like that, can also be black with dark striped shadows. Female hindwings have blue iridescent scales and a marginal orange spot. Females have a marginal spotted row on the underside of the forewing.

Honey Locust (*Gleditsia triacanthos*)
Robert H. Mohlenbrock @ USDA-NRCS PLANTS Database / USDA NRCS. 1995. Northeast wetland flora: Field office guide to plant species. Northeast National Technical Center, Chester.

Honey Locust (*Gleditsia triacanthos*)

Also Known As: *Gleditsia triacanthos var. inermis*

Plant Description: Growing 30 to 75 feet tall, the honey locust has yellow-green leaves and non-showy greenish flowers. Leaves are feather-like and compound with a yellow fall color. Flowers bloom between May and June. Seedpods go from red-green to a maroon-brown as they age. It is a perennial.

Growing Guide: Plant a honey locust in partial shade with a moist soil that is nearly neutral in pH. It is both cold and heat tolerant. Propagate by seed or cuttings. Seed should have 1 to 2 hours of sulfuric acid scarification.

Interesting Facts: The pulp has been dried and ground by Southeastern indigenous people for use as a sweetener.

Warnings: This is a prickly thorny plant. It can be prone to cankers, mites, and Mimosa webworm invaders.

Southern Distribution: Alabama, Arkansas, Florida, Georgia, Kentucky, Louisiana, Mississippi, North Carolina, South Carolina, Tennessee, Texas, Virginia, and West Virginia.

Classification: Family *Fabaceae* – Pea family

Genus *Gleditsia* L. – locust

Species *Gleditsia triacanthos* L. – honey locust

Butterflies and Moths Attracted: It is a food source for the Silver-spotted Skipper (*Epargyreus clarus*). It is a larval host to the Bicolored Honey Locust Moth (*Sphingicampa bicolor*) and the Bisected Honey Locust Moth (*Sphingicampa bisecta*). With a secure NatureServe Global Status rating of G5, the silver-spotted skipper butterfly isn't near extinction. It has a wingspan of 1 3/4-inches to 2 5/8-inches. There are forewing gold spots and a hindwing with a silver band on this black or brown-winged butterfly. The hindwing of a silver-spotted skipper will be lobed.

The bicolored honey locust moth has a G5, or secure, NatureServe Global Status and a wingspan of 1 7/8-inches to 2 5/8-inches. Wings can be brown-yellow, red-orange, or red-brown on the upperside with up to two white cell spots and a postmedian line. Forewing and hindwing can have scattered black specks. It is very variable.

With a NatureServe Global Status of G5, or secure, the bisected honey locust moth has a wingspan of 2 1/16-inches to 2 15/16-inches. Males may be yellow or orange but females are mostly yellow. There are hindwing red patches and a nearly-straight postmedian line on the forewing. Males do not have black specks but females do.

American Holly (*Ilex opaca*)
Robert H. Mohlenbrock @ USDA-NRCS PLANTS Database / USDA NRCS. 1995. Northeast wetland flora: Field office guide to plant species. Northeast National Technical Center, Chester.

American Holly (*Ilex opaca*)

Also Known As: Christmas Holly

Plant Description: Growing from 25 to 60 feet high, this evergreen has matte dark green leaves. Foliage is spiny. Branches are stiff and have light gray bark. Females will have red berries that are bright in color.

Growing Guide: This holly can grow in any lighting, from full sun to full shade, and wet or dry acidic soil. Soils should be well drained. It has both a cold and heat tolerance. Propagate by seed or semi-hardwood cuttings. Seed should be scarified or have double stratification.

Interesting Facts: The wood of this holly has been used in woodworking.

Warnings: All Ilex plants are somewhat toxic and should not be ingested.

Southern Distribution: Alabama, Arkansas, Florida, Georgia, Kentucky, Louisiana, Mississippi, North Carolina, South Carolina, Tennessee, Texas, Virginia, and West Virginia.

Classification: Family *Aquifoliaceae* – Holly family

Genus *Ilex* L. – holly

Species *Ilex opaca* Aiton – American holly

Butterflies and Moths Attracted: It is a larval host to Henry's Elfin (*Callophrys henrici*). This butterfly has a G5 secure NatureServe Global Status rating and a wingspan between 1-inch and 1 1/4-inches. It has dark brown wings with typically an orange hue at the hindwing tail and the forewing outer margin. It is a tailed butterfly.

Yaupon (*Ilex vomitoria*)
Larry Allain @ USDA-NRCS PLANTS Database

Yaupon (*Ilex vomitoria*)

Also Known As: Cassina, Yaupon Holly

Plant Description: Growing 12 to 45 feet tall with an average of 25 feet high, the yaupon is a small tree, with leaves under 1 1/2-inches long. There is pale gray bark marked with white patches. Berries are red and bright and long lasting with white blooms lasting from April to May.

Growing Guide: Plant in any lighting and with a moist or dry well-drained soil. It is both cold and heat tolerant. Propagate by seed or semi-hardwood cuttings. Seed may need 1 to 2 months of warm stratification and then 2 to 3 months of cold stratification.

Interesting Facts: Leaves and twigs from a yaupon can be made into a caffeinated tea. Berries are useful in holiday decorations.

Warnings: For berries, you'll need a male and a female plant specimen.

Southern Distribution: Alabama, Arkansas, Florida, Georgia, Louisiana, Mississippi, North Carolina, South Carolina, Texas, and Virginia.

Classification: Family *Aquifoliaceae* – Holly family

Genus *Ilex* L. – holly

Species *Ilex vomitoria* Aiton – yaupon

Butterflies and Moths Attracted: It is a larval host to Henry's Elfin (*Callophrys henrici*). This butterfly has a G5 secure NatureServe Global Status rating and a wingspan between 1-inch and 1 1/4-inches. It has dark brown wings with typically an orange hue at the hindwing tail and the forewing outer margin. It is a tailed butterfly.

Tuliptree (*Liriodendron tulipifera*)
Larry Allain @ USDA-NRCS PLANTS Database

Tuliptree (*Liriodendron tulipifera*)

Also Known As: Tulip Poplar

Plant Description: It can get up to 150 feet tall with a straight trunk. Leaves are waxy and green, turning bright gold in the fall season. Foliage is star-shaped. Flowers are yellow-orange and look like a tulip. Seed heads are cone-like.

Growing Guide: Tuliptree is fine in any lighting with a moist acidic soil. It is a fast grower in rich well-drained soils. Propagate by seeds or cuttings. Seeds can be sown fresh in the fall or after two to three months of stratification in the spring.

Interesting Facts: Early Pioneers once used the tuliptree as a cholera treatment. First Nations people made a worming remedy from the inner bark.

Warnings: This tree doesn't like to be near pavement, in confined planters or beds, or grown in compacted soil.

Southern Distribution: Alabama, Arkansas, Florida, Georgia, Kentucky, Louisiana, Mississippi, North Carolina, South Carolina, Tennessee, Texas, Virginia, and West Virginia.

Classification: Family *Magnoliaceae* – Magnolia family

Genus *Liriodendron* L. – tuliptree

Species *Liriodendron tulipifera* L. – tuliptree

Butterflies and Moths Attracted: It is a larval host for the Eastern Tiger Swallowtail (*Papilio glaucus*) and the Tuliptree Silkmoth (*Callosamia angulifera*). Secure with a NatureServe Global Status of G5, the Eastern tiger swallowtail has a wingspan between 3 5/8-inches and 6 1/2-inches. Male butterflies have dark tiger-striped yellow wings. Females, while they may be colored like that, can also be black with dark striped shadows. Female hindwings have blue iridescent scales and a marginal orange spot. Females have a marginal spotted row on the underside of the forewing.

With a secure G5 NatureServe Global Status, the tuliptree silkmoth has a wingspan of 3 1/8-inches to 4 5/16-inches. Males are brown with white cells spots in an angle. There is a pink band on the underside. Females are yellow-brown with white cell spots in an angle. There is a dark red hindwing underside. Both are darker in the summer season.

Red Mulberry (*Morus rubra*)

Also Known As: Moral

Plant Description: This tree grows under 60 feet tall with a broad crown and long ovate leaves. Green foliage turns bright yellow in the fall season. Fruits look like blackberries and the flowers are catkins.

Growing Guide: It grows fine in any lighting and soil. Propagate by seed, layering, or cuttings. Seed should have two to three months of cold stratification.

Interesting Facts: The red mulberry fruits have been used by the Native Americans as a food, either eaten fresh or made into cakes and preserves.

Warnings: The sap and the raw fruits have a low toxicity and can give cramps and hallucinations.

Southern Distribution: Alabama, Arkansas, Florida, Georgia, Kentucky, Louisiana, Mississippi, North Carolina, South Carolina, Tennessee, Texas, Virginia, and West Virginia.

Classification: Family *Moraceae* – Mulberry family

Genus *Morus* L. – mulberry

Species *Morus rubra* L. – red mulberry

Butterflies and Moths Attracted: It is a larval host to the Mourning Cloak (*Nymphalis antiopa*). The mourning cloak butterfly has a secure ranking with a NatureServe Global status of G5, it also has a wingspan between 2 1/4-inches and 4-inches. There are irregular borders and short projections on the wings, with a purple-black upperside. There is a yellow border and blue spots on a row on the outer margin of the wings.

Redbay (*Persea borbonia*)
Larry Allain @ USDA-NRCS PLANTS Database

Redbay (*Persea borbonia*)

Also Known As: Red Bay

Plant Description: Growing up to 65 feet tall, this evergreen short tree has aromatic foliage. Leaves are leathery and dark green. Flowers are pale yellow and in panicles. Fruits are dark-blue or black.

Growing Guide: Grow a redbay in partial shade with a moist acidic soil. Seed should be sown after collection or after a month of cold-moist stratification if planting in spring.

Interesting Facts: Though bitter, the fruits are eaten by birds.

Warnings: It is prone to Laurel wilt disease.

Southern Distribution: Alabama, Arkansas, Florida, Georgia, Louisiana, Mississippi, North Carolina, South Carolina, and Texas.

Classification: Family *Lauraceae* – Laurel family

Genus *Persea* Mill. – bay

Species *Persea borbonia* (L.) Spreng. – redbay

Butterflies and Moths Attracted: It is a larval host to the Palamedes Swallowtail (*Papilio palamedes*) and the Spicebush Swallowtail (*Papilio troilus*) butterflies. Having a secure G5 NatureServe Global Status, the Palamedes swallowtail has a winspan of 4 1/2-inches to 5 1/8-inches. It is dark with a yellow band on postmedian and yellow on the tails. The hindwing has a yellow basal stripe and yellow-orange crescents.

With a G5, secure, NatureServe Global Status, the spicebush swallowtail has a wingspan between 3-inches and 4-inches. The forewing is mainly black with ivory spots on the upperside, while the hindwing upperside can have bluish scales on the female and blue-greenish scales on the male. The upperside to the hindwing also has a costal margin orange spot. There are pale green spots on the hindwing underside.

Loblolly Pine (*Pinus taeda*)

Also Known As: Old Field Pine, Rosemary Pine, Bull Pine

Plant Description: Usually growing to 60 feet tall it can reach up to 110 feet high. This large fragrant pine tree has dark green needles and gray scaly bark. It will fruit in a cone.

Growing Guide: Plant this pine in partial shade conditions with a moist sandy soil. It is cold tolerant. Propagate by seed sown in the fall without treatment.

Interesting Facts: It is native to 15 states, is the fastest growing southern pine, and is used for pulpwood and lumber.

Warnings: This tree can be prone to pine beetles and rust.

Southern Distribution: Alabama, Arkansas, Florida, Georgia, Kentucky, Louisiana, Mississippi, North Carolina, South Carolina, Tennessee, Texas, and Virginia.

Classification: Family *Pinaceae* – Pine family

Genus *Pinus* L. – pine

Species *Pinus taeda* L. – loblolly pine

Butterflies and Moths Attracted: It is a larval host to the Southern Pine Sphinx (*Lapara coniferarum*). With no reported NatureServe Global Status as of this writing and a wingspan between 2-inches and 2 1/4-inches, the southern pine sphinx is gray with one to three black dashes by the center of the wing. There is a brown-gray hindwing. Females are bigger than the males.

Virginia Pine (*Pinus virginiana*)

Also Known As: Jersey Pine

Plant Description: This straggling pine grows 15 to 40 feet high and may get flat-topped when mature. The trunk is red-brown and the limbs are irregular. Needles are short and cones are sharp.

Growing Guide: Grow this pine in full sun and with a moist well-drained soil. It does well in poor soils. Propagate by seed that has not been treated.

Interesting Facts: This is one of the main woods used for lumber and pulpwood.

Southern Distribution: Alabama, Georgia, Kentucky, Mississippi, North Carolina, South Carolina, Tennessee, and Virginia

Classification: Family *Pinaceae* – Pine family

Genus *Pinus* L. – pine

Species *Pinus virginiana* Mill. – Virginia pine

Butterflies and Moths Attracted: It is a larval host to the Eastern Pine Elfin (*Callophrys niphon*). The eastern pine elfin has a secure G5 NatureServe Global Status and a wingspan between 1-inch and 1 1/4-inches. It is dark brown and tailess with dark brown on the underside. There is a gray band and black crescents on the hindwing. Females will have dark borders.

Eastern Cottonwood (*Populus deltoides*)
Jennifer Anderson @ USDA-NRCS PLANTS Database

Eastern Cottonwood (*Populus deltoides*)

Also Known As: Necklace Poplar

Plant Description: This stout tree grows up to 100 feet high. It has a large canopy, deciduous medium green leaves, and clusters of flowers. Leaves are papery and turn yellow in the fall. Flowers come March and April and are without petals. Seeds have cotton-like hairs.

Growing Guide: It grows in any lighting and soil moisture. Soil should be well-drained and nearly neutral in pH. It is cold tolerant. Propagate by semi-hardwood cuttings or by seed.

Interesting Facts: It is also called the necklace poplar because of the seed capsules resemblance to a pearl necklace. In addition, a tea was once made from the bark for heartburn, scurvy, and as a female tonic. The bark may have had some actual medicinal use because of it containing an aspirin-like compound.

Warnings: The tree is prone to borers and cankers.

Southern Distribution: Alabama, Arkansas, Florida, Georgia, Kentucky, Louisiana, Mississippi, North Carolina, South Carolina, Tennessee, Texas, Virginia, and West Virginia.

Classification: Family *Salicaceae* – Willow family

Genus *Populus* L. – cottonwood

Species *Populus deltoides* Bartram ex Marsh. – eastern cottonwood

Butterflies and Moths Attracted: It is a larval host to the Mourning Cloak (*Nymphalis antiopa*), and the Viceroy (*Limenitis archippus*). The mourning cloak butterfly has a secure ranking with a NatureServe Global status of G5; it also has a wingspan between 2 1/4-inches and 4-inches. There are irregular borders and short projections on the wings, with a purple-black upperside. There is a yellow border and blue spots on a row on the outer margin of the wings.

Secure with a NatureServe Global Status of G5, the viceroy has a wingspan of 2 1/2-inches to 3 3/8-inches. It mimics the monarch in coloring, with and orange and black upperside (rarely brown instead of orange, depending on location). The viceroy has hindwing black lines and white dots in a row on the black marginal band.

Wafer Ash (*Ptelea trifoliata*)

Also Known As: Hop Tree, Common Hoptree

Plant Description: This tree reaches 20 to 26 feet high with a round crown. It has a slender trunk. Bark, leaves, and twigs have a musky lemon smell. Leaves are deciduous and dark green, turning yellow in the fall. Small flowers are in clusters and green-white in color. Fruits are broad-winged samaras.

Growing Guide: It grows in any lighting conditions or soil types as long as the pH is nearly neutral. This tree does best in moist well-drained soils. Propagate by seed, softwood cuttings, or semi-hardwood cuttings. Seed needs to have three months of stratification.

Interesting Facts: The fruits can be used as a hop substitute in beer making.

Southern Distribution: Alabama, Arkansas, Florida, Georgia, Kentucky, Louisiana, Mississippi, North Carolina, South Carolina, Tennessee, Texas, Virginia, and West Virginia.

Classification: Family *Rutaceae* – Rue family

Genus *Ptelea* L. – hoptree

Species *Ptelea trifoliata* L. – common hoptree

Butterflies and Moths Attracted: It is a larval host to the Giant Swallowtail (*Papilio cresphontes*) and the Eastern Tiger Swallowtail (*Papilio glaucus*). The giant swallowtail has a G5, or secure, NatureServe Global Status and a wingspan between 4-inches and 6 1/4-inches. Underside is yellow with black borders and yellow spots while upperside is black with a diagonal yellow spot band on forewing. Tail is black with a yellow dot.

Secure with a NatureServe Global Status of G5, the Eastern tiger swallowtail has a wingspan between 3 5/8-inches and 6 1/2-inches. Male butterflies have dark tiger-striped yellow wings. Females, while they may be colored like that, can also be black with dark striped shadows. Female hindwings have blue iridescent scales and a marginal orange spot. Females have a marginal spotted row on the underside of the forewing.

It grows 20 to 26 feet high with a round crown. It has a slender trunk. Bark, leaves, and twigs have a musky lemon smell. Leaves are deciduous and dark green, turning yellow in the fall. Small flowers are in clusters and green-white in color. Fruits are broad-winged samaras.

Southern Red Oak (*Quercus falcata*)
Robert H. Mohlenbrock @ USDA-NRCS PLANTS Database / USDA NRCS. 1995. Northeast wetland flora: Field office guide to plant species. Northeast National Technical Center, Chester.

Southern Red Oak (*Quercus falcata*)

Also Known As: Spanish Oak

Plant Description: While it can grow up to 70 feet tall, it is generally shorter. The trunk is straight and its bark is smooth gray when young and furrowed dark gray when mature. Leaves are thin and green but turn red-brown in the fall. Acorns are thing with a red-brown cup.

Growing Guide: Grow this tree in partial shade and dry soil. Propagate by seed that have been cold-moist stratified for one to three months prior to planting. It is cold tolerant and long-lived.

Interesting Facts: The Spanish oak name comes from it commonly being found in areas where there were early Spanish colonies.

Southern Distribution: Alabama, Arkansas, Florida, Georgia, Kentucky, Louisiana, Mississippi, North Carolina, South Carolina, Tennessee, Texas, Virginia, and West Virginia.

Classification: Family *Fagaceae* – Beech family

Genus *Quercus* L. – oak

Species *Quercus falcata* Michx. – southern red oak

Butterflies and Moths Attracted: It is a larval host to the Banded Hairstreak (*Satyrium calanus*) and the White M Hairstreak (*Parrhasius m-album*). The banded hairstreak has a NatureServe Global Status of G5, secure, and a wingspan of one-inch to 1 1/2-inches wide. There is a short and a long tail on the brown hindwing. Underside is darker with dark colored dashes with white edges. There is a blue tail spot and some orange near the tailspot.

The white m hairstreak has a NatureServe Global Status of G5, or secure, and a wingspan of 1 1/4-inches to 1 5/8-inches. It has a black bordered iridescent blue color to the upperside and a gray-brown for the underside. It is tailed. There is a black lined white line on postmedian and a white "m" or "w" by the tail.

Blackjack Oak (*Quercus marilandica*)

Plant Description: This oak tree grows 30 to 50 feet high with leaves that have shiny tops and a hairy rust-yellow color below. The bark is dark and furrowed. The glossy green leaves turn red in the fall. Fruits are acorns, broad and round.

Growing Guide: Grow this oak in partial shade with a dry soil. It does well even in poor soils. It is slow-growing but cold tolerant. Propagate by acorns.

Interesting Facts: Native Americans have used the blackjack oak as a dysentery remedy. Other uses include having the leaves as cigarette wrappers and using the wood for charcoal, railroad ties, and firewood.

Warnings: It is prone to oak wilt.

Southern Distribution: Alabama, Arkansas, Florida, Georgia, Kentucky, Mississippi, Louisiana, North Carolina, South Carolina, Tennessee, Texas, Virginia, and West Virginia.

Classification: Family *Fagaceae* – Beech family

Genus *Quercus* L. – oak

Species *Quercus marilandica* Münchh. – blackjack oak

Butterflies and Moths Attracted: It is a larval host to the White M Hairstreak (*Parrhasius m-album*) and Horace's Duskywing (*Erynnis horatius*). The white m hairstreak has a NatureServe Global Status of G5, or secure, and a wingspan of 1 1/4-inches to 1 5/8-inches. It has a black bordered iridescent blue color to the upperside and a gray-brown for the underside. It is tailed. There is a black lined white line on postmedian and a white "m" or "w" by the tail.

With a secure G5 NatureServe Global Status and a wingspan of 1 7/16-inches to 1 15/16-inches, Horace's duskywing has brown fringes. Males are dark brown and females are light brown. Females have large transparent spots and a contrasting pattern. There are two spots to the hindwing underside. Males have yellow scent scales on a costal fold and females have scent scales on the abdomen.

Horace's Duskywing
(C) Mark Dreiling of Santee, CA

Swamp Chestnut Oak (*Quercus michauxii*)
Robert H. Mohlenbrock @ USDA-NRCS PLANTS Database / USDA SCS. 1989. Midwest wetland flora: Field office illustrated guide to plant species. Midwest National Technical Center, Lincoln.

Swamp Chestnut Oak (*Quercus michauxii*)

Also Known As: Cow Oak, Basket Oak, *Quercus prinus*

Plant Description: An oak with a narrow crown, this grows 60 to 100 feet high. It has a light gray bark and simple leaves. Leaves are shiny and green, turning yellow and then red in the fall. Fruits are tan brown acorns.

Growing Guide: *Quercus michauxii* prefers partial shade and a moist soil. It is drought tolerant and does best in deep rich soil. Propagate by acorns.

Interesting Facts: This is one of the best oak trees to plant for fall color. Cows also love the acorns which is how it gets the cow oak name.

Southern Distribution: Alabama, Arkansas, Florida, Georgia, Kentucky, Louisiana, Mississippi, North Carolina, South Carolina, Tennessee, Texas, and Virginia.

Classification: Family *Fagaceae* – Beech family

Genus *Quercus* L. – oak

Species *Quercus michauxii* Nutt. – swamp chestnut oak

Butterflies and Moths Attracted: It is a larval host to the White M Hairstreak (*Parrhasius m-album*). The white m hairstreak has a NatureServe Global Status of G5, or secure, and a wingspan of 1 1/4-inches to 1 5/8-inches. It has a black bordered iridescent blue color to the upperside and a gray-brown for the underside. It is tailed. There is a black lined white line on postmedian and a white "m" or "w" by the tail.

Chinkapin Oak (*Quercus muehlenbergii*)

Also Known As: *Quercus acuminata, Quercus prinoides, Quercus alexanderi, Quercus prinoides var. acuminata*

Plant Description: This oak grows under 60 feet tall with light gray scaly bark. Twigs are smooth, gray at the beginning and maturing to brown. Leaves are shiny on the top and dull on the underside. Flowers aren't showy and the fruit is an acorn.

Growing Guide: This oak grows in full sun or partial shade with a dry alkaline soil. Propagate by seedlings or acorns after scarification.

Interesting Facts: Acorns are edible after boiling to release the tannins that are stored in the nut. These acorns can be ground to use as a coffee substitute, or made into a flour. Some use it to thicken soups or fry it in a batter.

Warnings: Young leaves and acorns have a low toxicity and can give constipation symptoms as well as stomachaches and excessive thirst.

Southern Distribution: Alabama, Arkansas, Florida, Georgia, Kentucky, Louisiana, Mississippi, North Carolina, South Carolina, Tennessee, Texas, Virginia, and West Virginia.

Classification: Family *Fagaceae* – Beech family

Genus *Quercus* L. – oak

Species *Quercus muehlenbergii* Engelm. – chinkapin oak

Butterflies and Moths Attracted: It is a larval host to the Gray Hairstreak (*Strymon melinus*). The gray hairstreak has a secure rating, or G5, for its NatureServe Global Status and a wingspan between 7/8-inch and 1 3/8-inches. It is blue-gray with a red spot near the tail. There is one tail. The spring or fall variable of the butterfly is gray on the underside while the summer variable is pale gray. There is a white postmedian line that is bordered in orange.

Pin Oak (*Quercus palustris*)
Robert H. Mohlenbrock @ USDA-NRCS PLANTS Database / USDA SCS. 1991. Southern wetland flora: Field office guide to plant species. South National Technical Center, Fort Worth.

Pin Oak (*Quercus palustris*)

Plant Description: This straight tree grows 60 to 70 feet high with slender twigs. Leaves are dark green and get dark red by the fall. This fine textured tree grows in a narrow form. Fruits will be nuts.

Growing Guide: Plant this oak in any type of lighting conditions and in wet or moist acidic soil. It is fine in poorly drained soils. Propagate by seed that has been freshly collected or after 1 to 1 ½ months of stratification.

Interesting Facts: Insects make galls in the tree that can be steeped with water and iron filings to make a black dye.

Warnings: This oak can be prone to iron chlorosis if it is in alkaline soil.

Southern Distribution: Arkansas, Georgia, Kentucky, Mississippi, North Carolina, South Carolina, Tennessee, Virginia, and West Virginia

Classification: Family *Fagaceae* – Beech family

Genus *Quercus* L. – oak

Species *Quercus palustris* Münchh. – pin oak

Butterflies and Moths Attracted: It is a larval host to the Gray Hairstreak (*Strymon melinus*). The gray hairstreak has a secure rating, or G5, for its NatureServe Global Status and a wingspan between 7/8-inch and 1 3/8-inches. It is blue-gray with a red spot near the tail. There is one tail. The spring or fall variable of the butterfly is gray on the underside while the summer variable is pale gray. There is a white postmedian line that is bordered in orange.

Willow Oak (*Quercus phellos*)
Robert H. Mohlenbrock @ USDA-NRCS PLANTS Database / USDA NRCS. 1995. Northeast wetland flora: Field office guide to plant species. Northeast National Technical Center, Chester.

Willow Oak (*Quercus phellos*)

Plant Description: Growing up to 100 feet high, this tree has a straight trunk and narrow leaves. Foliage is long and tapered, green in color. During the fall season the leaves will go from bright green to yellow or russet. There is gray or red-brown bark. Acorns are nearly completely round.

Growing Guide: The willow oak prefers partial shade locations and a moist soil. It is propagated by seed that is fresh from collection or after one to two months of stratification.

Interesting Facts: It makes for a great shade tree but it may grow too large to be near houses.

Southern Distribution: Alabama, Arkansas, Florida, Georgia, Kentucky, Louisiana, Mississippi, North Carolina, South Carolina, Tennessee, Texas, and Virginia.

Classification: Family *Fagaceae* – Beech family

Genus *Quercus* L. – oak

Species *Quercus phellos* L. – willow oak

Butterflies and Moths Attracted: It is a larval host to the White M Hairstreak (*Parrhasius m-album*). The white m hairstreak has a NatureServe Global Status of G5, or secure, and a wingspan of 1 1/4-inches to 1 5/8-inches. It has a black bordered iridescent blue color to the upperside and a gray-brown for the underside. It is tailed. There is a black lined white line on postmedian and a white "m" or "w" by the tail.

Northern Red Oak (*Quercus rubra*)

Also Known As: *Quercus rubra var. rubra, Quercus borealis var. maxima*

Plant Description: Growing up to 120 feet tall but usually staying between 75 feet to 100 feet. Bark is dark in color with bristle-tipped leaf lobes. Green leaves are simple and foliage is dense. There is great red, gold-orange, and russet fall color.

Growing Guide: The Northern red oak should be planted in full sun or partial shade with a moist or dry acidic soil. Soil should be well drained. Propagate by seed that are sown fresh or that have gone through stratification.

Interesting Facts: Nuts can be ground to make flour or roasted and ground to make a coffee substitute.

Warnings: This particular oak is prone to the oak wilt disease and can get chlorosis in high pH soils. Young leaves and the nuts can be poisonous, but are edible after the tannins in the nuts have been boiled out.

Southern Distribution: Alabama, Arkansas, Georgia, Kentucky, Louisiana, Mississippi, North Carolina, South Carolina, Tennessee, Virginia, and West Virginia.

Classification: Family *Fagaceae* – Beech family

Genus *Quercus* L. – oak

Species *Quercus rubra* L. – northern red oak

Butterflies and Moths Attracted: It is a larval host to the Gray Hairstreak (*Strymon melinus*). The gray hairstreak has a secure rating, or G5, for its NatureServe Global Status and a wingspan between 7/8-inch and 1 3/8-inches. It is blue-gray with a red spot near the tail. There is one tail. The spring or fall variable of the butterfly is gray on the underside while the summer variable is pale gray. There is a white postmedian line that is bordered in orange.

Coastal Live Oak (*Quercus virginiana*)
Larry Allain @ USDA-NRCS PLANTS Database

Coastal Live Oak (*Quercus virginiana*)

Also Known As: Live Oak, Southern Live Oak

Plant Description: This southern Spanish-moss laced favorite grows 40 to 80 feet high and 60 to 100 feet wide. Leaves are waxy and dark green. It grows in a tapering trunk form with large irregular limbs, typically draping the ground at times. It appears evergreen, but leaves fall off right when the new leaves are starting to emerge.

Growing Guide: Plant this in full sun or partial shade and in moist soil. It is heat tolerant. Propagate from seed without need of pretreatment.

Interesting Facts: Live oak wood was once used as ship building wood. It has also been a dysentery herbal remedy from the Houma people.

Warnings: Long stretches of freezing weather can damage this oak tree. It is prone to oak wilt and to chestnut blight disease.

Southern Distribution: Alabama, Florida, Georgia, Louisiana, Mississippi, North Carolina, South Carolina, Texas, and Virginia.

Classification: Family *Fagaceae* – Beech family

Genus Quercus L. – oak

Species *Quercus virginiana* Mill. – coastal live oak

Butterflies and Moths Attracted: It is a larval host to the White M Hairstreak (*Parrhasius m-album*) and the Consular Oakworm moth (*Anisota consularis*). The white m hairstreak has a NatureServe Global Status of G5, or secure, and a wingspan of 1 1/4-inches to 1 5/8-inches. It has a black bordered iridescent blue color to the upperside and a gray-brown for the underside. It is tailed. There is a black lined white line on postmedian and a white "m" or "w" by the tail.

The consular oakworm moth has an apparently secure G4 NatureServe Global Status and a wingspan between 1 1/4-inches and 2 5/8-inches. Females are red-orange or brown-orange with black specks scattered about and white cell spot on forewing. Males are brown-red with black specks scattered about and a white cell spot and clear patch on forewing.

Pussy Willow (*Salix discolor*)
Robert H. Mohlenbrock @ USDA-NRCS PLANTS Database / USDA SCS. 1989. Midwest wetland flora: Field office illustrated guide to plant species. Midwest National Technical Center, Lincoln.

Pussy Willow (*Salix discolor*)

Plant Description: Growing up to 20 feet high, this can be a small tree or a shrub form. It has several trunks and a dark gray bark that is scaly. Catkins come before the leaves appear, and are silver-gray. Leaves are bright green, deciduous, and are shiny. The flowers have buds that have soft hairs and give it the cat moniker in its name. Bloom season is between February and March.

Growing Guide: The pussy willow prefers full sun and a moist soil that is nearly neutral in pH. It grows quickly. Propagate by root cuttings, semi-hardwood cuttings, seed, and hardwood cuttings. Seed should be fresh and untreated when sown.

Interesting Facts: *Salix discolor* has the first willow catkins that appear in the spring.

Warnings: This tree is prone to wind damage and insect damage.

Southern Distribution: Kentucky, North Carolina, Virginia, and West Virginia.

Classification: Family *Salicaceae* – Willow family

Genus *Salix* L. – willow

Species *Salix discolor* Muhl. – pussy willow

Butterflies and Moths Attracted: It is a larval host to the Mourning Cloak (*Nymphalis antiopa*) and the Viceroy (*Limenitis archippus*). The mourning cloak butterfly has a secure ranking with a NatureServe Global status of G5; it also has a wingspan between 2 1/4-inches and 4-inches. There are irregular borders and short projections on the wings, with a purple-black upperside. There is a yellow border and blue spots on a row on the outer margin of the wings.

Secure with a NatureServe Global Status of G5, the viceroy has a wingspan of 2 1/2-inches to 3 3/8-inches. It mimics the monarch in coloring, with and orange and black upperside (rarely brown instead of orange, depending on location). The viceroy has hindwing black lines and white dots in a row on the black marginal band.

Black Willow (*Salix nigra*)
Larry Allain @ USDA-NRCS PLANTS Database

Black Willow (*Salix nigra*)

Also Known As: Gulf Black Willow

Plant Description: Growing 10 to 60 feet high, this fast growing tree has an open crown. They have long narrow leaves and bright yellow-green twigs and catkins. Clustered flowers are yellowish and appear March to April. Black willow has a furrowed bark and silky-haired seeds.

Growing Guide: It prefers to grow in any lighting with a moist or wet soil. Propagate by stem cuttings, seed, or root cuttings. Seed should be collected when the capsule are drying and yellow-brown in color.

Interesting Facts: The wood from the black willow has been made into boxes, pulpwood, doors, furniture, and cabinetry. It was made into charcoal that was used when making gunpowder during the American Revolution. Other uses for it include a medicinal tonic to purge the blood that was made from the root bark.

Warnings: This is a short-lived tree that is prone to both wind and insect damage.

Southern Distribution: Alabama, Arkansas, Florida, Georgia, Kentucky, Louisiana, Mississippi, North Carolina, South Carolina, Tennessee, Texas, Virginia, and West Virginia.

Classification: Family *Salicaceae*– Willow family

Genus *Salix* L.– willow

Species *Salix nigra* Marsh.– black willow

Butterflies and Moths Attracted: It is a larval host to the Mourning Cloak (*Nymphalis antiopa*). The mourning cloak butterfly has a secure ranking with a NatureServe Global status of G5, it also has a wingspan between 2 1/4-inches and 4-inches. There are irregular borders and short projections on the wings, with a purple-black upperside. There is a yellow border and blue spots on a row on the outer margin of the wings.

Sassafras (*Sassafras albidum*)
Larry Allain @ USDA-NRCS PLANTS Database

Sassafras (*Sassafras albidum*)

Also Known As: *Sassafras sassafras*

Plant Description: Growing 35 to 50 feet tall with deciduous green leaves and yellow-green flowers, the sassafras is also aromatic. Leaves will be bright green and oval in shape, with a great display of fall color. Its bark has deep furrows. Flowers are in clustered balls, blooming between March and May. Fruits are dark blue, nearly black.

Growing Guide: Sassafras can be grown in any lighting with moist acidic soil. Propagate by seed, root cuttings, or by suckers. Seed should have 1 to 2 months of cold stratification.

Interesting Facts: Its roots can be made into a tea and a jelly made from strong tea. The roots also give the oil of sassafras which is used as a fragrance.

Warnings: The bark contains safrole, which is poisonous. It also can be prone to chlorosis if the pH of the soil is too high.

Southern Distribution: Alabama, Florida, Georgia, Kentucky, Louisiana, Mississippi, North Carolina, South Carolina, Tennessee, Texas, Virginia, and West Virginia.

Classification: Family *Lauraceae* – Laurel family

Genus *Sassafras* Nees & Eberm. – sassafras

Species *Sassafras albidum* (Nutt.) Nees – sassafras

Butterflies and Moths Attracted: It is a food source for the Spicebush Swallowtail (*Papilio troilus*) and the Promethea Silkmoth (*Callosamia promethea*). With a G5, secure, NatureServe Global Status, the spicebush swallowtail has a wingspan between 3-inches and 4-inches. The forewing is mainly black with ivory spots on the upperside, while the hindwing upperside can have bluish scales on the female and blue-greenish scales on the male. The upperside to the hindwing also has a costal margin orange spot. There are pale green spots on the hindwing underside.

With a G5 NatureServe Global Status, the Promethea silkmoth has a wingspan of 2 15/16-inches to 3 3/4-inches. Females are dark-brown or red-brown and have tan cell spots and tan borders. Males are black with tan borders, pink on the forewing tip near the eyespots, and have light tan lines on their postmedian.

Winged Elm (*Ulmus alata*)

Plant Description: Growing 30 to 40 feet tall, this perennial tree has dark green ovate leaves that turn yellow in the fall. These deciduous leaves are simple and alternate. There are yellow or green blooms from February through April. Fruits are brown samaras.

Growing Guide: The winged elm should be planted in partial shade and a dry soil. It is cold tolerant. Propagate by softwood cuttings or by seed. Seed should be sown in the spring or in the fall after stratification. Use a rooting compound if propagating with cuttings.

Interesting Facts: Native Americans used winged elm inner bark as a remedy for diarrhea and to ease the pain of childbirth.

Warnings: It is prone to Dutch elm disease and powdery mildew.

Southern Distribution: Alabama, Arkansas, Florida, Georgia, Kentucky, Louisiana, Mississippi, North Carolina, South Carolina, Tennessee, Texas, and Virginia.

Classification: Family *Ulmaceae* – Elm family

Genus *Ulmus* L. – elm

Species *Ulmus alata* Michx. – winged elm

Butterflies and Moths Attracted: It is a larval host to the Question Mark (*Polygonia interrogationis*). The question mark butterfly has a G5, or secure, NatureServe Global Status and a wingspan between 2 1/4-inches and 3-inches. It is red-orange with black spots and a hooked forewing. There is a light brown underside with a pearl-white question mark in center of the hindwing. Winter butterflies have a longer tail than summer butterflies and have a hindwing upperside that is more orange than the blacker summer form.

American Elm (*Ulmus americana*)
USDA-NRCS PLANTS Database / Herman, D.E., et al. 1996. North Dakota tree handbook. USDA NRCS ND State Soil Conservation Committee; NDSU Extension and Western Area Power Administration, Bismarck.

American Elm (*Ulmus americana*)

Plant Description: Growing in a vase-like form, this tree gets 60 to 80 feet high with dark green leaves. Foliage has a variable fall color. Branches grow in a spreading form. Fruits are samaras.

Growing Guide: Grow this elm tree in full sun or partial shade with a moist nearly neutral pH soil. Propagate by cuttings or by seed.

Interesting Facts: It is a favorite wood for fruit and cheese crates due to the fact it is nearly odorless.

Warnings: This tree is prone to Dutch elm disease.

Southern Distribution: Alabama, Arkansas, Florida, Georgia, Kentucky, Louisiana, Mississippi, North Carolina, South Carolina, Tennessee, Texas, Virginia, and West Virginia.

Classification: Family *Ulmaceae* – Elm family

Genus *Ulmus* L. – elm

Species *Ulmus americana* L. – American elm

Butterflies and Moths Attracted: It is a larval host to Eastern Comma (*Polygonia comma*), Mourning Cloak (*Nymphalis antiopa*), Painted Lady (*Vanessa cardui*), Question Mark (*Polygonia interrogationis*). The eastern comma has a secure G5 NatureServe Global Status and a wingspan of 1 3/4-inches to 2 1/2-inches. It has a dark spotted brown-orange forewing upperside and a dark spot on the edge center. There are hindwing projections and a brown underside. Hindwing has a white or silver comma at both ends.

The mourning cloak butterfly has a secure ranking with a NatureServe Global status of G5, it also has a wingspan between 2 1/4-inches and 4-inches. There are irregular borders and short projections on the wings, with a purple-black upperside. There is a yellow border and blue spots on a row on the outer margin of the wings.

The painted lady is secure with a G5 NatureServe Global Status and has a wingspan between 2-inches and 2 7/8-inches. It has orange-brown wings with a darker base of the wings and an underside of black, brown, and gray. Undersides have four small eyespots. The forewing has a white edge bar and a black patch on apex. The hindwing has black spots in five rows and could have blue scales depending on butterfly.

The question mark butterfly has a G5, or secure, NatureServe Global Status and a wingspan between 2 1/4-inches and 3-inches. It is red-orange with black spots and a hooked forewing. There is a light brown underside with a pearl-white question mark in center of the hindwing. Winter butterflies have a longer tail than summer butterflies and have a hindwing upperside that is more orange than the blacker summer form.

Slippery Elm (*Ulmus rubra*)
Robert H. Mohlenbrock @ USDA-NRCS PLANTS Database / USDA SCS. 1991. Southern wetland flora: Field office guide to plant species. South National Technical Center, Fort Worth.

Slippery Elm (*Ulmus rubra*)

Also Known As: *Ulmus fulva*, Red Elm

Plant Description: This perennial tree grows 40 to 60 feet high with dark green leaves and samara fruits. The leaves are fuzzy underneath. There is a open form to the tree, with a slight vase shape.

Growing Guide: It grows in full sun or partial shade with a moist alkaline soil. Propagate by seed that is sown fresh or after two to three months of stratification. Layering of shoots or suckers is another form of propagation.

Interesting Facts: The inner bark can be dried and used as a cough medicine or poultice in folklore medicine. This glue-like section is fragrant and thick.

Warnings: This can be considered weedy and it is prone to Dutch elm disease.

Southern Distribution: Alabama, Arkansas, Florida, Georgia, Kentucky, Louisiana, Mississippi, North Carolina, South Carolina, Tennessee, Texas, Virginia, and West Virginia.

Classification: Family *Ulmaceae* – Elm family

Genus *Ulmus* L. – elm

Species *Ulmus rubra* Muhl. – slippery elm

Butterflies and Moths Attracted: It is a larval host to the Question Mark (*Polygonia interrogationis*), and Mourning Cloak (*Nymphalis antiopa*). The question mark butterfly has a G5, or secure, NatureServe Global Status and a wingspan between 2 1/4-inches and 3-inches. It is red-orange with black spots and a hooked forewing. There is a light brown underside with a pearl-white question mark in center of the hindwing. Winter butterflies have a longer tail than summer butterflies and have a hindwing upperside that is more orange than the blacker summer form.

The mourning cloak butterfly has a secure ranking with a NatureServe Global status of G5, it also has a wingspan between 2 1/4-inches and 4-inches. There are irregular borders and short projections on the wings, with a purple-black upperside. There is a yellow border and blue spots on a row on the outer margin of the wings.

Farkleberry (*Vaccinium arboreum*)
Robert H. Mohlenbrock @ USDA-NRCS PLANTS Database / USDA SCS. 1991. Southern wetland flora: Field office guide to plant species. South National Technical Center, Fort Worth.

Farkleberry (*Vaccinium arboreum*)

Also Known As: Sparkleberry, Tree Sparkleberry

Plant Description: Growing 12 to 15 feet tall on average but able to reach heights of 25 feet, the farkleberry has coarse deciduous leaves and black berries. White bell-like flowers are fragrant. Blooming season is between March and June. Leaves are dark green, shiny, and turn deep red in the fall. It has exfoliating bark and crooked branches.

Growing Guide: Plant this in partial shade with a dry soil. There is a tolerance to cold temperatures. Propagate by seed, hardwood cuttings, or by softwood cuttings. Seed will need stratification.

Interesting Facts: These seeds are eaten by wildlife even though they are not palatable to humans.

Warnings: It can be prone to chlorosis in soils with high alkalinity.

Southern Distribution: Alabama, Arkansas, Florida, Georgia, Kentucky, Louisiana, Mississippi, North Carolina, South Carolina, Tennessee, Texas, and Virginia.

Classification: Family *Ericaceae* – Heath family

Genus *Vaccinium* L. – blueberry

Species *Vaccinium arboreum* Marsh. – farkleberry

Butterflies and Moths Attracted: It is a larval host to the Striped Hairstreak (*Satyrium liparops*). Secure with a G5 NatureServe Global Status, the striped hairstreak has a wingspan between 1-inch and 1 1/2-inches. There is a long and a short tail. There are dark brown wings with white stripes and an orange-topped blue tail spot.

Hercules' Club (*Zanthoxylum clava-herculis*)
Larry Allain @ USDA-NRCS PLANTS Database

Hercules' Club (*Zanthoxylum clava-herculis*)

Plant Description: This is a spiny tree with aromatic foliage that grows 30 to 40 feet tall. It has spreading branches and blooms yellow-green from March through April. Flowers are in racemes. Fruits are red-brown or black inside a brown husk.

Growing Guide: Grow in full sun conditions with a dry soil. Propagate by seed,suckers, or by cuttings. Seed will require three months of cold stratification. Scarification is optional.

Interesting Facts: The bark has been used as a toothache home remedy. It is said that chewing the bark can numb the mouth.

Southern Distribution: Alabama, Arkansas, Florida, Georgia, Louisiana, Mississippi, North Carolina, South Carolina, Texas, and Virginia.

Classification: Family *Rutaceae* – Rue family

Genus *Zanthoxylum* L. – pricklyash

Species *Zanthoxylum clava-herculis* L. – Hercules' club

Butterflies and Moths Attracted: It is a larval host to the Giant Swallowtail (*Papilio cresphontes*). The giant swallowtail has a G5, or secure, NatureServe Global Status and a wingspan between 4-inches and 6 1/4-inches. Underside is yellow with black borders and yellow spots while upperside is black with a diagonal yellow spot band on forewing. Tail is black with a yellow dot.

Chapter Six: Native Shrubs

Again, it is important to keep native plants in your garden and landscaping whenever possible. Plants species are becoming extinct at a fast rate - quicker than most people are aware of. Every year a new species is pushed to the brink while non-native ornamental plants are shipped into the country.

Native shrubs provide ground cover, wildlife refuge, and even edible berries for human consumption. While deciding which shrubs to incorporate into your garden, consider not only those that are beautiful, but those that can offer fruit for your family. Quite a few native plants have fruit - northern shrubs have cranberries or blueberries, even wild black raspberry can be placed in your garden.

The fruit from these shrubs are edible and add a splash of color to your lawn. A properly placed blueberry shrub is beautiful - there are even blueberries that aren't blue, but pink! These varieties may be hard to find, but are worth the effort of searching them out.

Native rose shrubs have lush foliage, gorgeous flowers, and in the late summer/ early fall, crimson rose hips beckon to birds that are wintering in your area. Did you know that rose hips contain a large amount of vitamin C? Not only is the native rose a beneficial addition to your garden and local animal population, it is great for your own health.

Another less talked about benefit to using local, native shrubs for your garden is that the choices are often very low cost, if not free. Check with your local county extension office to find out what plants are endangered in your area. If you come across someone that is digging up shrubs, you may be able to take them off their hands free (or even be paid to remove them) and add a special flair to your ornamental garden at a fraction of the cost of imported plants.

Indigo Bush (*Amorpha fruticosa*)
Jennifer Anderson @ USDA-NRCS PLANTS Database

Indigo Bush (*Amorpha fruticosa*)

Also Known As: False Indigo Bush, False Indigo, Desert False Indigo, *Amorpha fruticosa var. occidentalis*

Plant Description: Growing 6 to 10 feet tall, this deciduous shrub has a light airy growth pattern. Leaves are compound and finely textured. Flowers are dark blue or purple and small, growing on spike-like clusters. Blooms appear between April and June.

Growing Guide: Plant it in full sun or partial shade with moist soil. It adapts to the pH of the soil. There is a tolerance to cold. Propagate by softwood cuttings, seed, or hardwood cuttings. Seed should be acid scarified for 5 to 8 minutes.

Warnings: In the northeast U.S., it can be weedy or invasive.

Southern Distribution: Alabama, Arkansas, Florida, Georgia, Kentucky, Louisiana, Mississippi, North Carolina, South Carolina, Tennessee, Texas, Virginia, and West Virginia.

Classification: Family *Fabaceae* – Pea family

Genus *Amorpha* L. – false indigo

Species *Amorpha fruticosa* L. – indigo bush

Butterflies and Moths Attracted: It is a larval host to the Silver-spotted Skipper (*Epargyreus clarus*), the Southern Dogface (*Zerene cesonia*), Gray Hairstreak (*Strymon melinus*), and the Hoary Edge (*Achalarus lyciades*) butterflies. With a secure NatureServe Global Status rating of G5, the silver-spotted skipper butterfly isn't near extinction. It has a wingspan of 1 3/4-inches to 2 5/8-inches. There are forewing gold spots and a hindwing with a silver band on this black or brown-winged butterfly. The hindwing of a silver-spotted skipper will be lobed.

The southern dogface has a secure G5 NatureServe Global Status and a wingspan between 2 1/8-inches and 3-inches. There is a black bordered yellow "dog's head" on the forewing upperside. Females have duller colors and more black. In summer, there is a yellow underside to the hindwing and in winter there is a black and pink mottled color.

The gray hairstreak has a secure rating, or G5, for its NatureServe Global Status and a wingspan between 7/8-inch and 1 3/8-inches. It is blue-gray with a red spot near the tail. There is one tail. The spring or fall variable of the butterfly is gray on the underside while the summer variable is pale gray. There is a white postmedian line that is bordered in orange.

The hoary edge has a G5, or secure, NatureServe Global Status and a wingspan between 1 3/4-inches and 1 15/16-inches. It is dark brown with a gold band that is transparent on the forewing center. There are checkered fringes and a black-brown hindwing underside with a silver-white band.

Gray Hairstreak
(C) Mark Dreiling of Santee, CA

Kinnikinnick (*Arctostaphylos uva-ursi*)

Also Known As: Red Bearberry

Plant Description: This evergreen shrub is native to Virginia and found only there in the South. It has leaves that look like paddles, yellow-green in spring turning dark-green and then red-purple by the fall. Flowers are clustered and small, pink or white in color, and are bell-like. Blooms will appear between March and June. Red berries last into the winter season. Bark is red, papery, and exfoliating.

Growing Guide: It prefers any type of lighting and moist or dry acidic soil. It is both cold and heat tolerant. Propagate by seed, layering, or by softwood cuttings. Seed should be treated with 3 to 6 hours of acid scarification, then 2 to 3 months of warm stratification, and then 2 to 3 months of cold stratification.

Interesting Facts: It was once used as a folklore remedy for kidney disease and urinary tract infections. Red bearberry has also been an astringent tea, a tobacco substitute, and a treatment for sexually transmitted diseases. It has an edible fruit that can make a cider-like drink.

Southern Distribution: Virginia.

Classification: Family *Ericaceae* – Heath family

Genus *Arctostaphylos* Adans. – manzanita

Species *Arctostaphylos uva-ursi* (L.) Spreng. – kinnikinnick

Butterflies and Moths Attracted: It is a larval host to the Hoary Elfin (*Callophrys polia*) in the states of Virginia and West Virgina. It is also a larval host to the Brown Elfin (*Callophrys augustinus*). The hoary elfin has a NatureServe Global Status of G5, or secure, and a wingspan between 7/8-inch and 1 1/8-inches. It is orange-brown on the upperside of the wings and brown on the underside. There is a frosted white outer margin of the forewing and a frosted light gray outer hindwing. It has no tails.

The brown elfin has a G5, or secure, NatureServe Global Status and a wingspan of 7/8-inch and 1 1/8-inches. Females are red-brown and males are gray-brown on their upperside and there are no tails. The hindwing is darker at the base and there is a chestnut brown underside with a dark line on postmedian.

New Jersey Tea (*Ceanothus americanus*)
Larry Allain @ USDA-NRCS PLANTS Database

New Jersey Tea (*Ceanothus americanus*)

Also Known As: Redroot

Plant Description: This small shrub grows up to 3 feet tall with deciduous grayish leaves. Flowers are white, small, and in clusters. It will bloom between March and April. There are many branches that grow in a spreading form.

Growing Guide: A New Jersey tea prefers partial shade to full shade with a moist or dry soil that is nearly neutral in pH. It is tolerant to cold weather. Propagate by seed, semi-hardwood cuttings, or softwood cuttings. Seed should put into hot water and then be in cool water for a day. There should then be 2 to 3 months of cold stratification.

Interesting Facts: This plant can recover quickly from fire due to deep roots. It also could have a tea made from the dried leaves, which was popular during the Revolutionary War.

Southern Distribution: Alabama, Arkansas, Florida, Georgia, Kentucky, Louisiana, Mississippi, North Carolina, South Carolina, Tennessee, Texas, Virginia, and West Virginia.

Classification: Family *Rhamnaceae* – Buckthorn family

Genus *Ceanothus* L. – ceanothus

Species *Ceanothus americanus* L. – New Jersey tea

Butterflies and Moths Attracted: It is a larval host to the Spring Azure (*Celastrina ladon*), Mottled Duskywing (*Erynnis martialis*), and the Summer Azure (*Celastrina neglecta*) butterflies. The spring azure has an apparent secure rating on NatureServe Global Status with a G4 rating. Its wingspan is between 7/8-inch and 1 3/8-inches. It has an upperside of a blue forewing and a gray-white underside.

With a NatureServe Global Status of G4, or apparently secure, the mottled duskywing has a wingspan between 1 1/8-inches and 1 5/8-inches. Wings have mottled colors and upperside bands. Young butterflies are iridescent purple with yellow scent scales on a male's costal fold and the female's scent scales on the abdominal segment.

The summer azure has a G5, or secure, NatureServe Global Status and a wingspan between 15/16-inch to 1 1/8-inches. Males are powder-blue with a white patch on hindwing while females have more white on the forewing and hindwing. Undersdies are gray or white with a dark zigzag line and black dots.

Redroot (*Ceanothus herbaceus*)
Clarence A. Rechenthin @ USDA-NRCS PLANTS Database

Redroot (*Ceanothus herbaceus*)

Also Known As: Jersey Tea, Inland Ceanothus, Prairie Redroot, Fuzzy Ceanothus, *Ceanothus ovatus*

Plant Description: A short perennial shrub, this plant grows 2 to 3 feet tall. Leaves have yellow veins and serrated margins. Foliage is dense. Flowers are in clusters, white, and bloom between March and July. Fruits are lobed capsules and are dark brown.

Growing Guide: Redroot prefers full sun conditions with a dry alkaline soil. Propagate by seeds, semi-hardwood cuttings, or softwood cuttings. Seed may need two to three months of stratification after a day of hot water scarification.

Interesting Facts: This tree can fix nitrogen from the atmosphere.

Southern Distribution: Kentucky, Texas, Virginia, and West Virginia.

Classification: Family *Rhamnaceae* – Buckthorn family

Genus *Ceanothus* L. – ceanothus

Species *Ceanothus herbaceus* Raf. – Jersey tea

Butterflies and Moths Attracted: The Butterflies and Moths of North America website lists it as a larval host to the Mottled Duskywing (*Erynnis martialis*). With a NatureServe Global Status of G4, or apparently secure, the mottled duskywing has a wingspan between 1 1/8-inches and 1 5/8-inches. Wings have mottled colors and upperside bands. Young butterflies are iridescent purple with yellow scent scales on a male's costal fold and the female's scent scales on the abdominal segment.

Common Buttonbush (*Cephalanthus occidentalis*)
Robert H. Mohlenbrock @ USDA-NRCS PLANTS Database / USDA SCS. 1989. Midwest wetland flora: Field office illustrated guide to plant species. Midwest National Technical Center, Lincoln.

Common Buttonbush (*Cephalanthus occidentalis*)

Also Known As: Button Willow, *Cephalanthus occidentalis var. californicus*

Plant Description: Growing 6 to 12 feet tall, this multi-stemmed shrub has dark green leaves and small clusters of flowers. Leaves are glossy above, dull below, and do not have good fall color. Blooms are white or pale pink and are in globes that look like pincushions. Fruits look like buttons. Blooms will appear between June and September.

Growing Guide: A common buttonbush should be planted in partial to full shade and wet or moist nearly neutral pH soil. It is cold tolerant. Propagate by untreated seed.

Interesting Facts: As early as 1735, the common buttonbush was being cultivated as a honey plant. In addition, it was a folklore remedy used by Native Americans for stomachaches and diarrhea.

Warnings: Foliage on the common buttonbush is poisonous.

Southern Distribution: Alabama, Arkansas, Florida, Georgia, Kentucky, Louisiana, Mississippi, North Carolina, South Carolina, Tennessee, Texas, Virginia, and West Virginia.

Classification: Family *Rubiaceae* – Madder family

Genus *Cephalanthus* L. – buttonbush

Species *Cephalanthus occidentalis* L. – common buttonbush

Butterflies and Moths Attracted: It is a food source to the Titan Sphinx (*Aellopos titan*) and the Hydrangea Sphinx (*Darapsa veriscolor*) moths. The titan sphinx has a GU, or unranked, rating on the NatureServe Global Status and a wingspan of 2 3/16-inches to 2 9/16-inches. It has dark brown wings and body with a white stripe on the abdomen. The upperside to the forewing has two bands of white spots and a black spot at the end of the cell. The upperside to the hindwing has costa and inner margin pale patches.

The hydrangea sphinx moth has a G4, or apparently secure, NatureServe Global Status and a wingspan between 2 1/4-inches and 3 1/8-inches. There are pink-white patches and dark lines on a green-brown forewing upperside. The hindwing upperside is yellow or red-brown with green-brown on the outer margin and white on the costal margin. There are green-brown and white areas on the inner margin.

Sweet Fern (*Comptonia peregrina*)

Also Known As: *Myrica aspleniifolia*

Plant Description: A small shrub, only reaching two to four feet high, it grows with a loose form. Aromatic olive-green leaves look fern-like and have rolled edges. Flowers are brown catkins. It will fruit as a nut wrapped in a bur-like husk.

Growing Guide: This plant prefers partial shade locations and a dry acidic soil. Propagate by root cuttings, stem cuttings, or by seed. Stem cuttings should be from young growth, approximately three inches long.

Interesting Facts: When crushed, the leaves are very aromatic since it is a member of the bayberry family of plants.

Southern Distribution: Georgia, Kentucky, North Carolina, South Carolina, Tennessee, Virginia, and West Virginia.

Classification: Family *Myricaceae* – Bayberry family

Genus *Comptonia* L'Hér. ex Aiton – sweet fern

Species *Comptonia peregrina* (L.) J.M. Coult. – sweet fern

Butterflies and Moths Attracted: It is a larval host to the Gray Hairstreak (*Strymon melinus*). The gray hairstreak has a secure rating, or G5, for its NatureServe Global Status and a wingspan between 7/8-inch and 1 3/8-inches. It is blue-gray with a red spot near the tail. There is one tail. The spring or fall variable of the butterfly is gray on the underside while the summer variable is pale gray. There is a white postmedian line that is bordered in orange.

Redosier Dogwood (*Cornus sericea*)
USDA-NRCS PLANTS Database / Herman, D.E., et al. 1996. North Dakota tree handbook. USDA NRCS ND State Soil Conservation Committee; NDSU Extension and Western Area Power Administration, Bismarck.

Redosier Dogwood (*Cornus sericea*)

Also Know As: Redosier, Red-twig Dogwood, *Cornus stolonifera*

Plant Description: Growing 6 to 12 feet high, this loose multi-stemmed shrub has clusters of cream-white flowers and white berries. Leaves are deciduous. Blooming season is between May and June.

Growing Guide: Grow a redosier dogwood in partial shade with a moist soil that is nearly neutral in pH. Soil should also be well-drained. Propagate by hardwood cuttings or by seed. Seed should have a two to three month cold-moist stratification period.

Interesting Facts: Not only does this shrub have colorful fall foliage but it also has scarlet branches in the winter season.

Warnings: This particular dogwood is prone to bagworms, scale, and twig blight.

Southern Distribution: Kentucky, Virginia, and West Virginia.

Classification: Family *Cornaceae* – Dogwood family

Genus *Cornus* L. – dogwood

Species *Cornus sericea* L. – redosier dogwood

Butterflies and Moths Attracted: It is a larval host to the Spring Azure (*Celastrina ladon*). The spring azure has an apparent secure rating on NatureServe Global Status with a G4 rating. Its wingspan is between 7/8-inch and 1 3/8-inches. It has an upperside of a blue forewing and a gray-white underside.

Beaked Hazelnut (*Corylus cornuta*)

Also Known As: *Corylus rostrata*, Beaked Filbert, *Corylus cornuta* var. *cornuta*

Plant Description: Growing four to eight feet high, this dense shrub has simple green leaves, yellow-brown catkins, and obscure flowers. It has beak-like nut husks. Foliage turns bright yellow and then a wine-red color as it matures. This perennial shrub grows in a mound form and can form thickets.

Growing Guide: This native prefers to grow in any lighting with a moist soil that is nearly neutral in pH. Propagate by seed or by separation of the roots.

Interesting Facts: The nuts are high in fat and protein. They are often browsed by squirrels, chipmunks, pheasant, blue jays, and ruffled grouse.

Southern Distribution: Alabama, Georgia, Mississippi, North Carolina, South Carolina, Tennessee, Virginia, and West Virginia.

Classification: Family *Betulaceae*– Birch family

Genus *Corylus* L.– hazelnut

Species *Corylus cornuta* Marsh.– beaked hazelnut

Butterflies and Moths Attracted: It is a larval host to the Early Hairstreak (*Erora laeta*) in the upper south portions of Georgia, Tennessee, Virginia, and the Carolinas. The early hairstreak has a G4, or apparently secure, NatureServe Global Status and a wingspan between 7/8-inch and 15/16-inch. It is blue and black and there are no tails. Females are bluer than the males. The hindwing has two bands of orange dots and a turquoise underside.

Northern Bush Honeysuckle (*Diervilla lonicera*)

Also Known As: *Diervilla diervilla*, Diervilla

Plant Description: Growing to three feet high, this small shrub has dark-green leaves and exfoliating bark. As the bark peels away there is orange inner bark that is revealed. Leaves will turn yellow and red in the fall. Flowers are small, yellow-green when they begin but maturing to red-purple or orange. Blooms are bell-like, occurring between June and August. It is a perennial.

Growing Guide: The Northern bush honeysuckle prefers to grow in partial shade or full shade conditions with a dry soil that is slightly acidic. Propagate by semi-hardwood cuttings, softwood cuttings, or by seed. Seed does not need pretreatment prior to sowing.

Warnings: It is a short-lived shrub.

Southern Distribution: Alabama, Georgia, North Carolina, Tennessee, Virginia, and West Virginia.

Classification: Family *Caprifoliaceae*– Honeysuckle family

Genus *Diervilla* Mill.– bush honeysuckle

Species *Diervilla lonicera* Mill.– northern bush honeysuckle

Butterflies and Moths Attracted: It is a larval host to the Snowberry Clearwing (*Hemaris diffinis*). The snowberry clearwing is secure, with a G5 NatureServe Global Status ranking. There is a 1 1/4-inch to 2-inch wingspan and it has a wide variety of looks, but typically looks like a bumblebee with clear wings.

Trailing Arbutus (*Epigaea repens*)

Also Known As: Mayflower, Plymouth Mayflower

Plant Description: This shrub only grows up to 6 inches tall and creeps along the ground. Leaves are evergreen and fragrant, with a leathery look. There are pink or white flowers, also aromatic, that are in clusters. Blooms will appear between March and May. Berries on the trailing arbutus are white and look like raspberries.

Growing Guide: This plant prefers partial shade or shade conditions with a moist well-drained acidic soil. Propagate by seed.

Interesting Facts: Believing this to be the first flower seen by Pilgrims after their first New England winter, it has been called a Plymouth Mayflower.

Warnings: Trailing arbutus will not tolerate drought, flood, or disturbances.

Southern Distribution: Alabama, Florida, Georgia, Kentucky, Mississippi, North Carolina, South Carolina, Tennessee, Virginia, and West Virginia.

Classification: Family *Ericaceae* – Heath family

Genus *Epigaea* L. – trailing arbutus

Species *Epigaea repens* L. – trailing arbutus

Butterflies and Moths Attracted: It is a larval host to the Hoary Elfin (*Callophrys polios*) in Virginia and West Virginia. The hoary elfin has a NatureServe Global Status of G5, or secure, and a wingspan between 7/8-inch and 1 1/8-inches. It is orange-brown on the upperside of the wings and brown on the underside. There is a frosted white outer margin of the forewing and a frosted light gray outer hindwing. It has no tails.

Wild Hydrangea (*Hydrangea arborescens*)

Also Known As: Sevenbark

Plant Description: Growing 3 to 6 feet tall, this small shrub grows into a mound. Leaves are deciduous. Flowers are in clusters, green-white in color, and delicate although massive. Blooms will be seen between June and August.

Growing Guide: Plant in a partial shade spot with a well-drained moist soil. Propagate by softwood cuttings or by seed. Seed does not need treating prior to planting, but they are very tiny.

Interesting Facts: At times, the blooms on this one will weigh enough to bring the stems to the ground level.

Warnings: Wild hydrangea is prone to winter dieback and sunscald. It can also get chlorosis in alkaline soil.

Southern Distribution: Alabama, Arkansas, Florida, Georgia, Kentucky, Louisiana, Mississippi, North Carolina, South Carolina, Tennessee, Virginia, and West Virginia.

Classification: Family *Hydrangeaceae* – Hydrangea family

Genus *Hydrangea* L. – hydrangea

Species *Hydrangea arborescens* L. – wild hydrangea

Butterflies and Moths Attracted: It is a larval host to the Hydrangea Sphinx (*Darapsa versicolor*) moth. The hydrangea sphinx moth has a G4, or apparently secure, NatureServe Global Status and a wingspan between 2 1/4-inches and 3 1/8-inches. There are pink-white patches and dark lines on a green-brown forewing upperside. The hindwing upperside is yellow or red-brown with green-brown on the outer margin and white on the costal margin. There are green-brown and white areas on the inner margin.

Sheep Laurel (*Kalmia angustifolia*)
Robert H. Mohlenbrock @ USDA-NRCS PLANTS Database / USDA NRCS. 1995. Northeast wetland flora: Field office guide to plant species. Northeast National Technical Center, Chester.

Sheep Laurel (*Kalmia angustifolia*)

Also Known As: Lambkill Kalmia

Plant Description: Growing up to 3 feet tall and 6 feet wide, this small evergreen shrub has deep pink saucer-like flowers and glossy leaves. Flowers are in clusters and the leaves are blue-green and turn red-green or purple in the fall season. Bloom season is between June and July.

Growing Guide: Grow a sheep laurel in partial shade with a wet and acidic soil. Deadheading the plant will ensure a better blooming season. Propagate by seed.

Interesting Facts: *Kalmia* plants are named for one of Linnaeus' students named Peter Kalm. He was an 18th century traveler and plant collector.

Warnings: This is a poisonous plant due to the resinoid andromedotoxin and the glycoside arbutin. If the plant is in alkaline soils, it can develop chlorosis due to an iron deficiency.

Southern Distribution: Virginia and West Virginia.

Classification: Family *Ericaceae* – Heath family

Genus *Kalmia* L. – laurel

Species *Kalmia angustifolia* L. – sheep laurel

Butterflies and Moths Attracted: It is a larval host to the Brown Elfin (*Callophrys augustinus*) butterfly. The brown elfin has a G5, or secure, NatureServe Global Status and a wingspan of 7/8-inch and 1 1/8-inches. Females are red-brown and males are gray-brown on their upperside and there are no tails. The hindwing is darker at the base and there is a chestnut brown underside with a dark line on postmedian.

Mountain Laurel (*Kalmia latifolia*)
W.D. Brush @ USDA-NRCS PLANTS Database

Mountain Laurel (*Kalmia latifolia*)

Also Known As: Calico Bush, *Kalmia latifolia var. laevipes*

Plant Description: With evergreen oval leaves and showy blooms, this broadleaf shrub grows between 12 and 20 feet tall. It has a single trunk. Flowers are bell-shaped and white or pink, clustered together. They will bloom between June and July. Foliage is leather-like and changes colors as the seasons change, from light green to darker and then to purple.

Growing Guide: Mountain laurel prefers partial shade and moist soils. Propagate by seed. Seed may be treated with cold moist stratification but is not required.

Interesting Facts: The wood has been used for handles and its knotty growths used for tobacco pipes.

Warnings: All parts of a mountain laurel are poisonous and contain the resinoid andromedotoxin and the glucoside arbutin.

Southern Distribution: Alabama, Florida, Georgia, Kentucky, Louisiana, Mississippi, North Carolina, South Carolina, Tennessee, Virginia, and West Virginia.

Classification: Family *Ericaceae* – Heath family

Genus *Kalmia* L. – laurel

Species *Kalmia latifolia* L. – mountain laurel

Butterflies and Moths Attracted: It is a larval host to the Laurel Sphinx (*Sphinx kalmiae*) moth. The laurel sphinx moth has G5, or secure, NatureServe Global Status and a wingspan between 2 15/16-inches to 4 1/16-inches. It is yellow-brown on forewing with an outer marginal white line and an inner marginal black patch. The tan hindwing has a black patch at base, black borders, and a black line on median.

Northern Spicebush (*Lindera benzoin*)

Plant Description: Growing 6 to 12 feet high, this deciduous shrub has light green branches and aromatic glossy simple leaves. Its green leaves turn gold-yellow in the fall. Flowers are pale yellow and in dense clusters of tiny blooms. Fruits are red and aromatic. Bloom season is in April.

Growing Guide: The northern spicebush can grow in any lighting and well-drained soil. Soil can be moist to dry. Propagate by seed that is sown fresh after collection or that has been stratified for three to four months prior to sowing.

Interesting Facts: Leaves and twigs can be fashioned into an aromatic tea. The fruits can be powdered and make a kitchen spice.

Southern Distribution: Alabama, Arkansas, Florida, Georgia, Kentucky, Mississippi, North Carolina, South Carolina, Tennessee, Texas, Virginia, and West Virginia.

Classification: Family *Lauraceae* – Laurel family

Genus *Lindera* Thunb. – spicebush

Species *Lindera benzoin* (L.) Blume – northern spicebush

Butterflies and Moths Attracted: It is a Spicebush Swallowtail (*Papilio troilus*), Promethea silkmoth (*Callosamia promethea*), and the Eastern Tiger Swallowtail (*Papilio glaucus*). With a G5, secure, NatureServe Global Status, the spicebush swallowtail has a wingspan between 3-inches and 4-inches. The forewing is mainly black with ivory spots on the upperside, while the hindwing upperside can have bluish scales on the female and blue-greenish scales on the male. The upperside to the hindwing also has a costal margin orange spot. There are pale green spots on the hindwing underside.

With a G5 NatureServe Global Status, the Promethea silkmoth has a wingspan of 2 15/16-inches to 3 3/4-inches. Females are dark-brown or red-brown and have tan cell spots and tan borders. Males are black with tan borders, pink on the forewing tip near the eyespots, and have light tan lines on their postmedian.

Secure with a NatureServe Global Status of G5, the Eastern tiger swallowtail has a wingspan between 3 5/8-inches and 6 1/2-inches. Male butterflies have dark tiger-striped yellow wings. Females, while they may be colored like that, can also be black with dark striped shadows. Female hindwings have blue iridescent scales and a marginal orange spot. Females have a marginal spotted row on the underside of the forewing.

Spicebush Swallowtail
(C) Mark Dreiling of Santee, CA

Wax Myrtle (*Morella cerifera*)
Larry Allain @ USDA-NRCS PLANTS Database

Wax Myrtle (*Morella cerifera*)

Also Known As: Candleberry, Southern Bayberry, *Myrica pusilla, Myrica cerifera*

Plant Description: Growing six to 12 feet tall on average with some specimens getting up to 20 feet, this spicy scented shrub has evergreen foliage and many trunks. There are olive-green leaves and pale blue berries on the female plants. Bark is nearly white, but is actually gray.

Growing Guide: Planting requires full sun or partial shade with a wet or moist acidic to nearly neutral pH soil. It is heat, drought, and flood tolerant. Propagate by seeds, semi-hardwood cuttings, and by softwood cuttings. Seed requires two to three months cold-moist stratification or direct sow into the ground during the fall season. Cuttings should be two to three inch sections.

Interesting Facts: If the temperature drops below zero degrees F the plant will defoliate and not re-leaf until the spring. In addition, berries on this can be boiled and used as a candle wax.

Warnings: This will need pruning to get into a tree shape.

Southern Distribution: Alabama, Arkansas, Florida, Georgia, Louisiana, Mississippi, South Carolina, North Carolina, Texas, Virginia, and West Virginia.

Classification: Family *Myricaceae* – Bayberry family

Genus *Morella* Lour. – bayberry

Species *Morella cerifera* (L.) Small – wax myrtle

Butterflies and Moths Attracted: It is a larval host to the Banded Hairstreak (*Satyrium calanus*) and the Red-banded Hairstreak (*Calycopis cecrops*) butterflies. The banded hairstreak has a NatureServe Global Status of G5, secure, and a wingspan of one-inch to 1 1/2-inches wide. There is a short and a long tail on the brown hindwing. Underside is darker with dark colored dashes with white edges. There is a blue tail spot and some orange near the tailspot.

The red-banded hairstreak is secure with a G5 NatureServe Global Status and has a wingspan of 7/8-inch to 1 1/4-inches. The hindwing has two tails and is blue, with a brown forewing. The underside is gray-brown with a white line with red-orange borders.

Banded Hairstreak
(C) Mark Dreiling of Santee, CA

Chokecherry (*Prunus virginiana*)
Sheri Hagwood @ USDA-NRCS PLANTS Database

Chokecherry (*Prunus virginiana*)

Plant Description: This large shrub grows 20 to 30 feet tall with deciduous green leaves and white clustered flowers. Fruits are red that mature to a dark purple. Flowers bloom between April and July.

Growing Guide: Chokecherries grow in any lighting with moist or dry soil that is nearly neutral in pH. It has a tolerance to cold. Propagate by seed, root cuttings, semi-hardwood cuttings, hardwood cuttings, and by softwood cuttings. Seed should be treated by 2 weeks of moist sand stratification then 2 to 3 months of cold stratification.

Interesting Facts: Native Americans used the roots and bark to make tonics for sedation. A tea was made for coughs, worms, stomachaches and malaria.

Warnings: The plant contains hydrocyanic acid, which is a toxin.

Southern Distribution: Arkansas, Georgia, Kentucky, North Carolina, Tennessee, Texas, Virginia, and West Virginia.

Classification: Family *Rosaceae* – Rose family

Genus *Prunus* L. – plum

Species *Prunus virginiana* L. – chokecherry

Butterflies and Moths Attracted: It is a larval host to the Small-eyed Sphinx moth (*Paonias myops*). It has a G5 secure NatureServe Global Status rating and a wingspan between 1 3/4-inches and 2 15/16-inches. They have indented forewings and variable colors. The wings are brown or black with a yellow patch that circles a black-rimmed eyespot on hindwing.

Fragrant Sumac (*Rhus aromatica*)
USDA-NRCS PLANTS Database / Herman, D.E., et al. 1996. North Dakota tree handbook. USDA NRCS ND State Soil Conservation Committee; NDSU Extension and Western Area Power Administration, Bismarck.

Fragrant Sumac (*Rhus aromatica*)

Also Known As: Aromatic Sumac, Polecat Bush, Lemon Sumac

Plant Description: This native plant grows 6 to 12 feet tall with blue-green glossy foliage. Leaves are coarse, toothed, and trifoliate. Flowers come before the leaves, and are yellow catkin-like blooms from April through June. In the fall, the shrub will go through colors of red, yellow, and orange. Berries are dark-red and last until March.

Growing Guide: Planting for a fragrant sumac is very easy. It tolerates any lighting or soil that is nearly neutral in pH. Even dry rocky soils are fine for it. Propagate by seed that has been scarified and stratified or by semi-hardwood cuttings. It can also be propagated by suckers. It is usually pest and disease free.

Interesting Facts: Berries are food for many animals and birds such as the Townsends Solitaires.

Warnings: Flowers and berries are only on female plants.

Southern Distribution: Alabama, Arkansas, Florida, Georgia, Kentucky, Louisiana, Mississippi, North Carolina, South Carolina, Tennessee, Texas, Virginia, West Virginia.

Classification: Family *Anacardiaceae* – Sumac family

Genus *Rhus* L. – sumac

Species *Rhus aromatica* Aiton – fragrant sumac

Butterflies and Moths Attracted: It is a larval host to the Red-banded Hairstreak (*Calycopis cecrops*) and the Banded Hairstreak (*Satyrium calanus*) butterflies. The red-banded hairstreak is secure with a G5 NatureServe Global Status and has a wingspan of 7/8-inch to 1 1/4-inches. The hindwing has two tails and is blue, with a brown forewing. The underside is gray-brown with a white line with red-orange borders.

The banded hairstreak has a NatureServe Global Status of G5, secure, and a wingspan of one-inch to 1 1/2-inches wide. There is a short and a long tail on the brown hindwing. Underside is darker with dark colored dashes with white edges. There is a blue tail spot and some orange near the tailspot.

Red-banded Hairstreak
(C) Mark Dreiling of Santee, CA

Winged Sumac (*Rhus copallinum*)

Also Known As: Shining Sumac, Flameleaf Sumac

Plant Description: Growing 20 to 35 feet high, the winged sumac has a short and crooked trunk. Leaves are dark-green and glossy. They'll turn red-purple in the fall season. Flowers are yellow-green and occur before dull red fruit clusters make an appearance. Flowers bloom between July and August.

Growing Guide: The winged sumac prefers to grow in full sun with a dry rocky soil. Propagate by seed, semi-hardwood cuttings, and division. Seed will need an hour or two of acidic scarification prior to sowing.

Interesting Facts: This sumac can be made into a beverage that is lemonade-like. It is also a food source for songbirds, small mammals, and gamebirds.

Southern Distribution: Alabama, Arkansas, Florida, Georgia, Kentucky, Louisiana, Mississippi, North Carolina, South Carolina, Tennessee, Texas, Virginia, and West Virginia.

Classification: Family *Anacardiaceae*– Sumac family

Genus *Rhus* L.– sumac

Species *Rhus copallinum* L.– winged sumac

Butterflies and Moths Attracted: It is a larval host to the Red-banded Hairstreak (*Calycopis cecrops*).The red-banded hairstreak is secure with a G5 NatureServe Global Status and has a wingspan of 7/8-inch to 1 1/4-inches. The hindwing has two tails and is blue, with a brown forewing. The underside is gray-brown with a white line with red-orange borders.

Staghorn Sumac (*Rhus typhina*)
USDA-NRCS PLANTS Database / Herman, D.E., et al. 1996. North Dakota tree handbook. USDA NRCS ND State Soil Conservation Committee; NDSU Extension and Western Area Power Administration, Bismarck.

Staghorn Sumac (*Rhus typhina*)

Also Known As: *Rhus hirta*

Plant Description: Growing 15 to 30 feet high, the staghorn sumac has large leaves that are bright green and compound. They make a great fall display. Twigs are velvety, trunks are crooked, and flowers are yellow-green. Fruits are red and in clusters. Bloom season is between June and July.

Growing Guide: This native is not very fussy in its growth needs. It will grow in any lighting and especially like a dry nearly neutral pH soil. Propagate by division, root cuttings, or by seed. Seed will need one to three hours of acid scarification and then a month of cold-moist stratification.

Interesting Facts: This native has been used to tan hides, using the tannin-rich bark, leaves, and fruit. It can also make a lemonade-like drink from the fruit. Its berries are a common food source for gray catbirds, American robins, eastern bluebirds, grouse, pheasant, and common crows.

Warnings: It can be easily damaged by lawn mowers and trimmers due to the thin bark.

Southern Distribution: Alabama, Georgia, Kentucky, Mississippi, North Carolina, South Carolina, Tennessee, Virginia, and West Virginia.

Classification: Family *Anacardiaceae*– Sumac family

Genus *Rhus* L.– sumac

Species *Rhus typhina* L.– staghorn sumac

Butterflies and Moths Attracted: It is a larval host to the Red-banded Hairstreak (*Calycopis cecrops*).The red-banded hairstreak is secure with a G5 NatureServe Global Status and has a wingspan of 7/8-inch to 1 1/4-inches. The hindwing has two tails and is blue, with a brown forewing. The underside is gray-brown with a white line with red-orange borders.

Prairie Willow (*Salix humilis*)
Robert H. Mohlenbrock @ USDA-NRCS PLANTS Database / USDA NRCS. 1995. Northeast wetland flora: Field office guide to plant species. Northeast National Technical Center, Chester.

Prairie Willow (*Salix humilis*)

Plant Description: Growing 6 to 12 feet high in a thicket-forming pattern, this shrub has wand-like branches and little if any fall color. Branches are yellow-brown and foliage is gray-green or blue-green. It will flower with green catkins prior to leaves forming.

Growing Guide: Plant the prairie willow in full sun with a wet or dry soil that is nearly neutral in pH. Propagate by stem cuttings, root cuttings or by seed. Seed should be untreated and sown fresh.

Warnings: This short-lived tree may be prone to wind damage.

Southern Distribution: Alabama, Arkansas, Florida, Georgia, Kentucky, Louisiana, Mississippi, North Carolina, South Carolina, Tennessee, Texas, Virginia, and West Virginia.

Classification: Family *Salicaceae* – Willow family

Genus *Salix* L. – willow

Species *Salix humilis* Marsh. – prairie willow

Butterflies and Moths Attracted: It is a larval host to the Green Comma (*Polygonia faunus*) butterfly in the states of Georgia, Tennessee, Kentucky, Alabama, South Carolina, North Carolina, West Virginia, and Virginia. The green comma is secure with a G5 NatureServe Global Status and has a wingspan between 1 3/4-inches and 2 1/1-inches. It is a variable butterfly, but generally has ragged wing edges with dark borders on a red-brown upperside and a yellow spotted border on the hindwing. There is a brown underside with a paler outer half and greenish spots on the submargin. There is a silver spot in the center of the hindwing that is shaped like a "C" or an "L".

Saw Palmetto (*Serenoa repens*)
Larry Allain @ USDA-NRCS PLANTS Database

Saw Palmetto (*Serenoa repens*)

Plant Description: This evergreen shrub grows up to 10 feet high and 6 feet wide. Leaves have saw-like toothed spines and are silver-white, green, or blue-green in color. Flowers are small and fragrant. The white blooms appear between May and July. There is an orange or black fruit.

Growing Guide: Plant a saw palmetto in partial shade and a well-drained soil. It can be propagated by seed but it is a slow germination.

Interesting Facts: It is known as the "prostate herb" for its purported affects as an herbal remedy for prostate trouble.

Southern Distribution: Alabama, Florida, Georgia, Louisiana, Mississippi, and South Carolina.

Classification: Family *Arecaceae* – Palm family

Genus *Serenoa* Hook. f. – serenoa

Species *Serenoa repens* (Bartram) Small – saw palmetto

Butterflies and Moths Attracted: It is a larval host to the Palmetto Skipper (*Euphyes arpa*). With a G3, or vulnerable, NatureServe Global Status, the Palmetto skipper has a wingspan between 1 5/8-inches and 1 15/16-inches. There is a bright orange head and yellow-orange hindwing underside. Males are red-yellow with a black hindwing, black borders, and a black 2-part stigma. Females are mostly black with red-yellow patches.

White Meadowsweet (*Spiraea alba*)
Robert H. Mohlenbrock @ USDA-NRCS PLANTS Database / USDA NRCS. 1995. Northeast wetland flora: Field office guide to plant species. Northeast National Technical Center, Chester.

White Meadowsweet (*Spiraea alba*)

Plant Description: *Spiraea alba* grows 3 to 6 feet high with finely textured stems. Yellow-green leaves will be gold-yellow by the fall. Flowers are white and small, appearing on terminal spikes between June and September. It is a dense and woody shrub.

Growing Guide: White meadowsweet prefers full sun or partial shade in a wet or moist well-drained soil that is nearly neutral in pH. Propagate by seed.

Interesting Facts: It is endangered in the state of Missouri.

Warnings: This shrub is going to be susceptible to fireblight, powdery mildew, scale, aphids, and leaf spots.

Southern Distribution: Kentucky, North Carolina, Tennessee, Virginia, and West Virginia.

Classification: Family *Rosaceae* – Rose family

Genus *Spiraea* L. – spirea

Species *Spiraea alba* Du Roi – white meadowsweet

Butterflies and Moths Attracted: It is a larval host to the Spring Azure (*Celastrina ladon*) butterfly. The spring azure has an apparent secure rating on NatureServe Global Status with a G4 rating. Its wingspan is between 7/8-inch and 1 3/8-inches. It has an upperside of a blue forewing and a gray-white underside.

Steeplebush (*Spiraea tomentosa*)
L. Scott Ranger @ USDA-NRCS PLANTS Database / USDA SCS. 1991. Southern wetland flora: Field office guide to plant species. South National Technical Center, Fort Worth

Steeplebush (*Spiraea tomentosa*)

Plant Description: Growing 3 to 6 feet high, this deciduous shrub has slender erect stems. Leaves are green and turn yellow in the fall. The orange or red-brown bark is exfoliating. Flowers are pink and in clusters, blooming between July and September.

Growing Guide: Spiraea tomentosa prefers moist acidic soil and full or partial sun conditions. Propagate by softwood cuttings or by seed. Seed will not need pretreatment nor do cuttings need rooting compound.

Interesting Facts: It gets its steeplebush name from the clusters of flowers being in a steeple shape.

Southern Distribution: Arkansas, Georgia, Kentucky, Louisiana, Mississippi, North Carolina, South Carolina, Tennessee, Virginia, and West Virginia.

Classification: Family *Rosaceae* – Rose family

Genus *Spiraea* L. – spirea

Species *Spiraea tomentosa* L. – steeplebush

Butterflies and Moths Attracted: It is a larval host plant to the Apple Sphinx moth (*Sphinx gordius*). It is has a G4, or apparently secure, NatureServe Global Status rating and a wingspan between 2 11/16-inches to 4 1/4-inches. It is a variable moth, typically black fringes on the forewing with some white marks. Fringes on the hindwing are white with some black marks. Black-bordered brown or brown-gray forewings are present with a gray or yellow-gray hindwing. The hindwings have a black border as well as a black median line.

Mapleleaf Viburnum (*Viburnum acerifolium*)

Also Known As: Arrow-wood, Maple-leaf Arrow-wood

Plant Description: Growing four to six feet high and three to four feet wide, this shrub is dense in its growth. There are deciduous leaves, bright green or dark green, that have good fall color. Flowers are white and in clusters, blooming between April and August. Berries are red or blue-black.

Growing Guide: Mapleleaf viburnum can be planted in any lighting and soil type as long as the soil is acidic. Propagate by seed that have been stratification.

Warnings: This plant is prone to Viburnum leaf beetle.

Southern Distribution: Alabama, Arkansas, Florida, Georgia, Kentucky, Louisiana, Mississippi, North Carolina, South Carolina, Tennessee, Texas, Virginia, and West Virginia.

Classification: Family *Caprifoliaceae* – Honeysuckle family

Genus *Viburnum* L. – viburnum

Species *Viburnum acerifolium* L. – mapleleaf viburnum

Butterflies and Moths Attracted: It is a larval host to the Spring Azure (*Celastrina ladon*) butterfly. The spring azure has an apparent secure rating on NatureServe Global Status with a G4 rating. Its wingspan is between 7/8-inch and 1 3/8-inches. It has an upperside of a blue forewing and a gray-white underside.

Southern Arrowwood (*Viburnum dentatum*)
USDA-NRCS PLANTS Database / Herman, D.E., et al. 1996. North Dakota tree handbook. USDA NRCS ND State Soil
Conservation Committee; NDSU Extension and Western Area Power Administration, Bismarck.

Southern Arrowwood (*Viburnum dentatum*)

Plant Description: This multi-stem shrub grows 6 to 8 feet high with a loose form. There are dark-green leaves that turn yellow before their wine-red fall color. Flowers are white and in clusters, appearing between May and July. Berries are dark blue.

Growing Guide: Grow a southern arrowwood in any lighting and with a moist acidic soil. Propagate by seed. If sown after collection they will not need pretreatment, but if stored before sowing it will need stratification. It is flood, disease, and insect resistant.

Interesting Facts: In addition to butterflies, this shrub also attracts such birds as the Gray Catbird, Eastern Bluebird, and the American Robin.

Southern Distribution: Alabama, Arkansas, Florida, Georgia, Kentucky, Louisiana, Mississippi, North Carolina, South Carolina, Tennessee, Texas, Virginia, and West Virginia.

Classification: Family *Caprifoliaceae* – Honeysuckle family

Genus *Viburnum* L. – viburnum

Species *Viburnum dentatum* L. – southern arrowwood

Butterflies and Moths Attracted: It is a larval host to the Spring Azure (*Celastrina ladon*) butterfly. The spring azure has an apparent secure rating on NatureServe Global Status with a G4 rating. Its wingspan is between 7/8-inch and 1 3/8-inches. It has an upperside of a blue forewing and a gray-white underside.

Hobblebush (*Viburnum lantanoides*)

Also Known As: *Viburnum alnifolium*

Plant Description: This perennial shrub grows 6 to 12 feet high. Flowers are fragrant clusters of white that look similar to hydrangeas. Foliage is medium green turning to bright red in fall. Fruits begin red and turn blue.

Growing Guide: It can grow in any lighting with a moist acidic soil and is shade tolerant. Propagate by seed collected after the fruits turn blue-black.

Interesting Facts: Small animals, songbirds, and gamebirds all use the fruit as a food source.

Southern Distribution: Georgia, North Carolina, Tennessee, and Virginia

Classification: Family *Caprifoliaceae* – Honeysuckle family

Genus *Viburnum* L. – viburnum

Species *Viburnum lantanoides* Michx. – hobblebush

Butterflies and Moths Attracted: It is a larval host to the Spring Azure (*Celastrina ladon*) butterfly. The spring azure has an apparent secure rating on NatureServe Global Status with a G4 rating. Its wingspan is between 7/8-inch and 1 3/8-inches. It has an upperside of a blue forewing and a gray-white underside.

Prickly Ash (*Zanthoxylum americanum*)

Also Known As: Toothache Tree

Plant Description: This perennial is aromatic and grows 12 to 25 feet high. Leaves are compound and dark green that turn yellow in the fall. Flowers are non-showy. Fruits start out red and age to black. It will grow in a dense thicket.

Growing Guide: Prickly ash prefers to grow in full sun environments where there is a nearly neutral soil pH. Propagate by seed. Seed needs two hours of acid scarification and then four months of cold-moist stratification.

Warnings: It is a thorny plant that can be weedy if not controlled.

Southern Distribution: Alabama, Arkansas, Florida, Georgia, Kentucky, Louisiana, North Carolina, South Carolina, Tennessee, Virginia, and West Virginia.

Classification: Family *Rutaceae*– Rue family

Genus *Zanthoxylum* L.– pricklyash

Species *Zanthoxylum americanum* Mill.– common pricklyash

Butterflies and Moths Attracted: It is a larval host to the Giant Swallowtail (*Papilio cresphontes*) and the Spicebush Swallowtail (*Papilio troilus*). The giant swallowtail has a G5, or secure, NatureServe Global Status and a wingspan between 4-inches and 6 1/4-inches. Underside is yellow with black borders and yellow spots while upperside is black with a diagonal yellow spot band on forewing. Tail is black with a yellow dot.

With a G5, secure, NatureServe Global Status, the spicebush swallowtail has a wingspan between 3-inches and 4-inches. The forewing is mainly black with ivory spots on the upperside, while the hindwing upperside can have bluish scales on the female and blue-greenish scales on the male. The upperside to the hindwing also has a costal margin orange spot. There are pale green spots on the hindwing underside.

Glossary

Native Plant Glossary

Acidic Soil – Soil that is less than 7.0 pH is considered acidic soil.

Alkaline Soil – Soil that is over 7.0 pH is considered alkaline soil.

Alternate – Leaves that are not directly across from one another on a stem are considered alternate.

Annual – Plants that have their entire lifecycle in one year are considered annuals.

Anther – The male part of a flower, which releases pollen, found on the upper section of a stamen.

Biennial – Plants that have their entire lifecycle in two years are considered biennial.

Bipinnate – Meaning divided once, bipinnate usually describes leaves.

Blade – A leaf's broad part.

Botanical Name – The Latin name, or scientific name, that is given to a plant.

Broadleaf Evergreen – Plants that keep their foliage year-round that also has non-needle-like leaves.

Capsule – Fruits that have two or more seeds that will eventually dry out and split open to release the seeds.

Class – There are three classes of plants; evergreens, broad-leaf evergreens, and decidous plants.

Common Name – The non-Latin name that plants are generally known by. These can differ wildly from region to region.

Compost – Organic items such as leaves and manure that will increase a soil's nutrients by breaking down.

Compound – Things that have more than a single part are called compound.

Conifer – Cone-forming plants that have evergreen needle-like foliage.

Cutting – A method of propagation where a section of plant is removed and used to root into a new plant.

Deadhead – Removing a seed head or bloom that is dead is called deadheading.

Deciduous – A plant that will lose its leaves at the end of the growing season is called deciduous.

Division – A method of propagation where the plant is put into sections and replanted into separate plants.

Drupe – Fruit of a plant that is fleshy tissue surrounding a seed.

Evergreen – A plant that will not lose their leaves when their growing season has ended.

Fronds – Large compound leaves that are usually from ferns and palms.

Glabrous – Smooth or hairless items.

Hardy – Plants said to be able to withstand cold and heat.

Lanceolate – Items that are narrow with a tapered end.

Lance-like – Items, like leaves, which are pointed at the tip and have enlongated shape.

Loam – A well-drained soil that has silt, clay and sand.

Mulch – Organic or inorganic items used to protect against weather, keep moisture in the soil, and prohibit weed growth.

Neutral – Describes soil that is 7.0 pH.

Opposite – Leaves that are directly across from each other on the stem.

Palmate – Radially lobed leaves that look like a wheel.

Perennial – Plants that have their entire lifecycle in three or more growing seasons.

pH – The 14 point scale showing acidic or alkaline, 7 being neutral.

Pinnate – Leaflets on a center line that are feather-like in structure.

Raceme – Clusters of flowers that are enlongated along a single stalk or main stem.

Rhizome – Woody or fleshy underground stems from a plant.

Samara – One-seed winged fruits that are dry and do not split open.

Serrated – Teeth along the margins of an item.

Specimen – Plants that have forms, fruit, flowers, or foliage that is desirable.

Stolon – Long horizontal stems that are on the ground's surface that root at tips and at nodes.

Succulent – Fleshy plants that conserve water in their stems.

Tender – Plants that cannot withstand cold or harsh heat.

Trifoliate – Items that have groups of three, such as leaves.

Butterfly Glossary

Cell – These are areas between the veins.

Costa – The upper portion or edge of wings.

Forewing – The wing closest to the head portion of the butterfly.

Hindwing – The rear wing.

Margin – the wing's edge.

NatureServe Global Status – A non-profit organization that ranks the rarity of butterflies and moths at a global level. There are six rankings; GU – unranked, G1 – critically imperiled, G2 – imperiled, G3 – very rare, G4 – apparently secure, and G5 – secure.

Scales – The shingle-like plates that cover the wings of a butterfly or moth that are formed by millions of modified hairs.

Stigma – Scent scale patch on the wings of the male butterflies that are very defined.

Veins – support for the wing membrane, the vein is tubular branching rods that go from margins of the wings to the base.

Wingspan – The distance from one tip of the forewing to the other forewing tip.

Appendix I: Specific Plants Arranged by Butterfly/Moth Species Attracted

Listed in order of book appearance.

Spring Azure (*Celastrina ladon*)
Black Cohosh (*Actaea racemosa var. racemosa*)
Coral Honeysuckle (*Lonicera sempervirens*)
Flowering Dogwood (*Cornus florida*)
New Jersey Tea (*Ceanothus americanus*)
Redosier Dogwood (*Cornus sericea*)
White Meadowsweet (*Spiraea alba*)
Mapleleaf Viburnum (*Viburnum acerifolium*)
Southern Arrowwood (*Viburnum dentatum*)
Hobblebush (*Viburnum lantanoides*)

American Lady (*Vanessa virginiensis*)
Pearly-everlasting (*Anaphalis margaritacea*)
Woman's Tobacco (*Antennaria plantaginifolia*)
Blunt-leaf Rabbit-tobacco (*Pseudognaphalium obtusifolium ssp. obtusifolium*)

Painted Lady (*Vanessa cardui*)
Pearly-everlasting (*Anaphalis margaritacea*)
Field Thistle (*Cirsium discolor*)
American Elm (*Ulmus americana*)

Silver-spotted Skipper (*Epargyreus clarus*)
Groundnut (*Apios americana*)
Showy Tick Trefoil (*Desmodium canadense*)
American Licorice (*Glycyrrhiza lepidota*)
American Wisteria (*Wisteria frutescens*)
Honey Locust (*Gleditsia triacanthos*)
Indigo Bush (*Amorpha fruticosa*)

Monarch (*Danaus plexippus*)
Spreading Dogbane (*Apocynum androsaemifolium*)
Swamp Milkweed (*Asclepias incarnata*)
Common Milkweed (*Asclepias syriaca*)
Butterflyweed (*Asclepias tuberosa*)
Whorled Milkweed (*Asclepias verticillata*)

Banded Hairstreak (*Satyrium calanus*)
Indian Hemp (*Apocynum cannabinum*)
Purple Passionflower (*Passiflora incarnata*)
Black Hickory (*Carya texana*)
Cockspur Hawthorn (*Crataegus crus-galli*)

Green Hawthorn (*Crataegus viridis*)
Southern Red Oak (*Quercus falcata*)
Wax Myrtle (*Morella cerifera*)
Fragrant Sumac (*Rhus aromatica*)

Columbine Duskywing (*Erynnis lucilius*)
Eastern Red Columbine (*Aquilegia canadensis*)

Pipevine Swallowtail (*Battus philenor*)
Virginia Snakeroot (*Aristolochia serpentaria*)
Common Dutchmanspipe (*Aristolochia tomentosa*)

Queen (*Danaus gilippus*)
Butterflyweed (*Asclepias tuberosa*)

White Peacock (*Anartia jatrophae*)
Coastal Water-hyssop (*Bacopa monnieri*)
Texas Frogfruit (*Phyla nodiflora*)

Frosted Elfin (*Callophrys irus*)
Blue Wild Indigo (*Baptisia australis*)
Horseflyweed (*Baptisia tinctoria*)
Sundial Lupine (*Lupinus perennis*)

Wild Indigo Duskywing (*Erynnis baptisiae*)
Blue Wild Indigo (*Baptisia australis*)
Horseflyweed (*Baptisia tinctoria*)
Sundial Lupine (*Lupinus perennis*)

Eastern Comma (*Polygonia comma*)
Bog Hemp (*Boehmeria cylindrica*)
American Elm (*Ulmus americana*)

Question Mark (*Polygonia interrogationis*)
Bog Hemp (*Boehmeria cylindrica*)
Sugar Hackberry (*Celtis laevigata*)
Common Hackberry (*Celtis occidentalis*)
Winged Elm (*Ulmus alata*)
American Elm (*Ulmus americana*)
Slippery Elm (*Ulmus rubra*)

Gray Hairstreak (*Strymon melinus*)
Winecup (*Callirhoe involucrata*)
Virginia Strawberry (*Fragaria virginiana*)
Cockspur Hawthorn (*Crataegus crus-galli*)
Green Hawthorn (*Crataegus viridis*)

Chinkapin Oak (*Quercus muehlenbergii*)
Pin Oak (*Quercus palustris*)
Northern Red Oak (*Quercus rubra*)
Indigo Bush (*Amorpha fruticosa*)
Sweet Fern (*Comptonia peregrina*)

Plebeian Sphinx (*Paratrea plebeja*)
Trumpet Creeper (*Campsis radicans*)

West Virginia White (*Pieris virginiensis*)
Cutleaf Toothwort (*Cardamine concatenata*)
Crinkleroot (*Cardamine diphylla*)

Western Pygmy-blue (*Brephidium exilis*)
Lambsquarters (*Chenopodium album*)

Cloudless Sulphur (*Phoebis sennae*)
Partridge Pea (*Chamaecrista fasciculata*)

Sleepy Orange (*Abaeis nicippe*)
Partridge Pea (*Chamaecrista fasciculata*)

Baltimore Checkerspot (*Euphydryas phaeton*)
White Turtlehead (*Chelone glabra*)
Allegheny Monkeyflower (*Mimulus ringens*)
Hairy Beardtongue (*Penstemon hirsutus*)

Little Metalmark (*Calephelis virginiensis*)
Yellow Thistle (*Cirsium horridulum*)

Swamp Metalmark (*Calephelis muticum*)
Swamp Thistle (*Cirsium muticum*)

Checkered White (*Pontia protodice*)
Rocky Mountain Beeplant (*Cleome serrulata*)

Goatweed Leafwing (*Anaea andria*)
Hogwort (*Croton capitatus*)
Prairie Tea (*Croton monanthogynus*)

Hoary Edge (*Achalarus lyciades*)
Showy Tick Trefoil (*Desmodium canadense*)
Indigo Bush (*Amorpha fruticosa*)

Texan Crescent (*Anthanassa texana*)
Branched Dicliptera (*Dicliptera brachiata*)

Northern Metalmark (*Calephelis borealis*)
Philadelphia Fleabane (*Erigeron philadelphicus*)

Pearl Crescent (*Phyciodes tharos*)
Bigleaf Aster (*Eurybia macrophylla*)
White Heath Aster (*Symphyotrichum ericoides var. ericoides*)
Smooth Blue Aster (*Symphyotrichum laeve var. laeve*)
New England Aster (*Symphyotrichum novae-angliae*)
Wavyleaf Aster (*Symphyotrichum undulatum*)

Grizzled Skipper (*Pyrgus centaureae*)
Virginia Strawberry (*Fragaria virginiana*)

Silvery Checkerspot (*Chlosyne nycteis*)
Thinleaf Sunflower (*Helianthus decapetalus*)

Black Swallowtail (*Papilio polyxenes*)
Common Cowparsnip (*Heracleum maximum*)
Golden Zizia (*Zizia aurea*)

Snowberry Clearwing (*Hemaris diffinis*)
Coral Honeysuckle (*Lonicera sempervirens*)
Northern Bush Honeysuckle (*Diervilla lonicera*)

Variegated Fritillary (*Euptoieta claudia*)
Common Moonseed (*Menispermum canadense*)
Purple Passionflower (*Passiflora incarnata*)
Birdfoot Violet (*Viola pedata*)

Common Buckeye (*Junonia coenia*)
Allegheny Monkeyflower (*Mimulus ringens*)
Texas Frogfruit (*Phyla nodiflora*)
Swamp Verbena (*Verbena hastata*)
Narrowleaf Vervain (*Verbena simplex*)

Virginia Creeper Sphinx (*Darapsa myron*)
Virginia Creeper (*Parthenocissus quinquefolia*)

Abbotts Sphinx Moth (*Sphecodina abbottii*)
Virginia Creeper (*Parthenocissus quinquefolia*)

Pandora Sphinx Moth (*Eumorpha pandorus*)
Virginia Creeper (*Parthenocissus quinquefolia*)

White-lined Sphinx Moth (*Hyles lineata*)

Virginia Creeper (*Parthenocissus quinquefolia*)

Zebra Heliconian (*Heliconius charithonia*)
Purple Passionflower (*Passiflora incarnata*)
Yellow Passion Vine (*Passiflora lutea*)

Gulf Fritillary (*Agraulis vanillae*)
Purple Passionflower (*Passiflora incarnata*)
Yellow Passion Vine (*Passiflora lutea*)

Julia Heliconian (*Dryas julia*)
Yellow Passion Vine (*Passiflora lutea*)

Phaon Crescent (*Phyciodes phaon*)
Texas Frogfruit (*Phyla nodiflora*)

Bordered Patch (*Chlosyne lacinia*)
Black-eyed Susan (*Rudbeckia hirta*)

Gorgone Checkerspot (*Chlosyne gorgone*)
Black-eyed Susan (*Rudbeckia hirta*)

Barred Yellow (*Eurema daira*)
Sidebeak Pencilflower (*Stylosanthes biflora*)

Regal Fritillary (*Speyeria idalia*)
Birdfoot Violet (*Viola pedata*)

Long-tailed Skipper (*Urbanus proteus*)
American Wisteria (*Wisteria frutescens*)

Zarucco Duskywing (*Erynnis zarucco*)
American Wisteria (*Wisteria frutescens*)

Delaware Skipper (*Anatrytone logan*)
Big Bluestem (*Andropogon gerardii*)
Switchgrass (*Panicum virgatum*)

Dusted Skipper (*Atrytonopsis hianna*)
Big Bluestem (*Andropogon gerardii*)
Little Bluestem (*Schizachyrium scoparium*)

Zabulon Skipper (*Poanes zabulon*)
Broomsedge Bluestem (*Andropogon virginicus*)
Canada Wildrye (*Elymus canadensis*)

Orange Skipperling (*Copaeodes aurantiaca*)
Sideoats Grama (*Bouteloua curtipendula*)

Bronze Roadside Skipper (*Amblyscirtes aenus*)
Sideoats Grama (*Bouteloua curtipendula*)
Inland Sea Oats (*Chasmanthium latifolium*)

Green Skipper (*Hesperia viridis*)
Buffalograss (*Bouteloua dactyloides*)
Hairy Grama (*Bouteloua hirsuta*)

Pepper and Salt Skipper (*Amblyscirtes hegon*)
Inland Sea Oats (*Chasmanthium latifolium*)
Indiangrass (*Sorghastrum nutans*)

Bells Roadside Skipper (*Amblyscirtes belli*)
Inland Sea Oats (*Chasmanthium latifolium*)

Salt Marsh Skipper (*Panoquina panoquin*)
Saltgrass (*Distichlis spicata*)

Least Skipper (*Ancyloxypha numitor*)
Rice Cut Grass (*Leersia oryzoides*)

Dotted Skipper (*Hesperia attalus*)
Switchgrass (*Panicum virgatum*)

Crossline Skipper (*Polites origenes*)
Little Bluestem (*Schizachyrium scoparium*

Indian Skipper (*Hesperia sassacus*)
Little Bluestem (*Schizachyrium scoparium*

Dion Skipper (*Euphyes dion*)
Woolgrass (*Scirpus cyperinus*)

Louisiana-eyed Silkmoth (*Automeris louisiana*)
Saltmarsh Cordgrass (*Spartina alterniflora*)

Crossline Skipper (*Polites origenes*)
Purpletop Tridens (*Tridens flavus*)

Little Glassywing (*Pompeius verna*)
Purpletop Tridens (*Tridens flavus*)

Common Wood Nymph (*Cercyonis pegala*)

Purpletop Tridens (*Tridens flavus*)

Broad-winged Skipper (*Poanes viator*)
Purpletop Tridens (*Tridens flavus*)

Byssus Skipper (*Problema byssus*).
Eastern Gamagrass (*Tripsacum dactyloides*)

Zebra Swallowtail (*Eurytides marcellus*)
Pawpaw (*Asimina triloba*)

Pawpaw Sphinx (*Dolba hyloeus*)
Pawpaw (*Asimina triloba*)

Green Comma (*Polygonia faunus*)
Cherry Birch (*Betula lenta*)
Prairie Willow (*Salix humilis*)

Eastern Tiger Swallowtail (*Papilio glaucus*)
American Hornbeam (*Carpinus caroliniana*)
White Ash (*Fraxinus americana*)
Green Ash (*Fraxinus pennsylvanica*)
Tuliptree (*Liriodendron tulipifera*)
Wafer Ash (*Ptelea trifoliata*)
Northern Spicebush (*Lindera benzoin*)

Striped Hairstreak (*Satyrium liparops*)
American Hornbeam (*Carpinus caroliniana*)
Cockspur Hawthorn (*Crataegus crus-galli*)
Farkleberry (*Vaccinium arboreum*)

Hackberry Emperor (*Asterocampa celtis*)
Sugar Hackberry (*Celtis laevigata*)
Common Hackberry (*Celtis occidentalis*)

Tawny Emperor (*Asterocampa clyton*)
Sugar Hackberry (*Celtis laevigata*)
Common Hackberry (*Celtis occidentalis*)

American Snout (*Libytheana carinenta*)
Sugar Hackberry (*Celtis laevigata*)
Common Hackberry (*Celtis occidentalis*)

Wild Cherry Sphinx moth (*Sphinx drupiferarum*)
Common Hackberry (*Celtis occidentalis*)

Red-banded Hairstreak (*Calycopis cecrops)*
Green Hawthorn (*Crataegus viridis*)
Wax Myrtle (*Morella cerifera*)
Fragrant Sumac (*Rhus aromatica*)
Winged Sumac (*Rhus copallinum*)
Staghorn Sumac (*Rhus typhina*)

Early Hairstreak (*Erora laeta*)
American Beech (*Fagus grandifolia*)
Beaked Hazelnut (*Corylus cornuta*)

Hickory Hairstreak (*Satyrium caryaevorus*)
White Ash (*Fraxinus americana*)

Mourning Cloak (*Nympalis antiopa*)
White Ash (*Fraxinus americana*)
Green Ash (*Fraxinus pennsylvanica*)
Red Mulberry (*Morus rubra*)
Eastern Cottonwood (*Populus deltoides*)
Pussy Willow (*Salix discolor*)
Black Willow (*Salix nigra*)
American Elm (*Ulmus americana*)
Slippery Elm (*Ulmus rubra*)

Viceroy (*Limenitis archippus*)
White Ash (*Fraxinus americana*)
Eastern Cottonwood (*Populus deltoides*)
Pussy Willow (*Salix discolor*)

Bicolored Honey Locust Moth (*Sphingicampa bicolor*)
Honey Locust (*Gleditsia triacanthos*)

Bisected Honey Locust Moth (*Sphingicampa bisecta*)
Honey Locust (*Gleditsia triacanthos*)

Henry's Elfin (*Callophrys henrici*)
American Holly (*Ilex opaca*)
Yaupon (*Ilex vomitoria*)

Tuliptree Silkmoth (*Callosamia angulifera*)
Tuliptree (*Liriodendron tulipifera*)

Palamedes Swallowtail (*Papilio palamedes*)
Redbay (*Persea borbonia*)

Spicebush Swallowtail (*Papilio troilus*)

Redbay (*Persea borbonia*)
Sassafras (*Sassafras albidum*)
Northern Spicebush (*Lindera benzoin*)
Prickly Ash (*Zanthoxylum americanum*)

Southern Pine Sphinx (*Lapara coniferarum*)
Loblolly Pine (*Pinus taeda*)

Eastern Pine Elfin (*Callophrys niphon*)
Virginia Pine (*Pinus virginiana*)

Giant Swallowtail (*Papilio cresphontes*)
Wafer Ash (*Ptelea trifoliata*)
Hercules' Club (*Zanthoxylum clava-herculis*)
Prickly Ash (*Zanthoxylum americanum*)

White M Hairstreak (*Parrhasius m-album*)
Southern Red Oak (*Quercus falcata*)
Blackjack Oak (*Quercus marilandica*)
Swamp Chestnut Oak (*Quercus michauxii*)
Willow Oak (*Quercus phellos*)
Coastal Live Oak (*Quercus virginiana*)

Horace's Duskywing (*Erynnis horatius*)
Blackjack Oak (*Quercus marilandica*)

Consular Oakworm moth (*Anisota consularis*)
Coastal Live Oak (*Quercus virginiana*)

Promethea Silkmoth (*Callosamia promethea*).
Sassafras (*Sassafras albidum*)
Northern Spicebush (*Lindera benzoin*)

Southern Dogface (*Zerene cesonia*)
Indigo Bush (*Amorpha fruticosa*)

Hoary Elfin (*Callophrys polia*)
Kinnikinnick (*Arctostaphylos uva-ursi*)
Trailing Arbutus (*Epigaea repens*)

Brown Elfin (*Callophrys augustinus*)
Kinnikinnick (*Arctostaphylos uva-ursi*)
Sheep Laurel (*Kalmia angustifolia*)

Mottled Duskywing (*Erynnis martialis*)
New Jersey Tea (*Ceanothus americanus*)

Redroot (*Ceanothus herbaceus*)

Summer Azure (*Celastrina neglecta*)
New Jersey Tea (*Ceanothus americanus*)

Titan Sphinx (*Aellopos titan*)
Common Buttonbush (*Cephalanthus occidentalis*)

Hydrangea Sphinx (*Darapsa veriscolor*)
Common Buttonbush (*Cephalanthus occidentalis*)
Wild Hydrangea (*Hydrangea arborescens*)

Laurel Sphinx (*Sphinx kalmiae*)
Mountain Laurel (*Kalmia latifolia*)

Small-eyed Sphinx moth (*Paonias myops*)
Chokecherry (*Prunus virginiana*)

Palmetto Skipper (*Euphyes arpa*)
Saw Palmetto (*Serenoa repens*)

Apple Sphinx moth (*Sphinx gordius*)
Steeplebush (*Spiraea tomentosa*)

Appendix II: Southern Native Plant and Butterfly Societies

Alabama
Alabama Wildflower Society
11120 Ben Clements Road
Northport, AL 35475
http://alwildflowers.org/

Arkansas
Arkansas Native Plant Society
P.O. Box 250250
Little Rock, AR 72225
http://www.anps.org/

Florida
Florida Native Plant Society
PO Box 278
Melbourne, FL 32902-0278
http://www.fnps.org

NABA-Hairstreak Chapter
Apalachicola Region (Central Florida Panhandle)
Sally Jue- President
E-mail: naba.hairstreak@gmail.com

NABA-North Central Florida
Kathy Malone- President
14572 NW 232 St.
High Springs, FL 32643
E-mail: zlongwing@aol.com
Web site: http://www.naba.org/chapters/nabancf/

NABA-Citrus County
Christine Small
4235 N. Lincoln Ave.
Beverly Hills, FL 34465
E-mail: butterflylady2@earthlink.net

NABA-Hernando-Pasco
Howard Wolf - President
1165 Divot Court
Spring Hill, FL 34608
E-mail: Howardhowolf@aol.com

NABA-Manasota

Connie Hodsdon
1512 22nd St. W.
Bradenton, FL 34205-4762
E-mail: chodsdon@tampabay.rr.com
Phone: (941) 807-2416 or (941) 795-3780

NABA-Pinellas County
Mary Ann Kuzmickas - President
E-mail: mkuzmickas@hotmail.com
Web site: http://freewebs.com/pinellasnaba/

NABA-Sarasota County Butterfly Club
Catherine LaBrie - President
1131 Blvd. of the Arts
Sarasota FL 34236
Contact: Beverly Bowen, NABA Liaison
E-mail: beverly@beverlybowen.com
Web site: http://www.sarasotabutterfly.org

NABA-Southwest Florida
Gayle Edwards - President
16185 Edgemont Dr.
Fort Myers, FL 33908
E-mail: mreds025@aol.com
Web site: http://sites.google.com/site/nabalongwings/

NABA-Atala Chapter (Palm Beach County)
Alana Edwards - President
3206 Palm Drive
Delray Beach, FL 33432
E-mail: rickandalana@bellsouth.net
Web site: http://www.naba.org/chapters/nabaac/

NABA-Broward County Butterfly Chapter
Janice Malkoff - President
E-mail: cycad49@aol.com
Web site: http://browardbutterflies.org

NABA-Miami Blue
Elane Nuehring - President
Phone: 305-666-5727
E-mail: emn6290@bellsouth.net
Dennis J. Olle - Vice-President
E-mail: dolle@carltonfields.com
Web site: http://www.miamiblue.org

Georgia
Georgia Native Plant Society
P.O. Box 422085
Atlanta, GA 30342-2085
http://www.gnps.org

Georgia Lepidoptera Society
14250 Phillips Circle, Alpharetta, GA 30201

Kentucky
Kentucky Native Plant Society
C/O Department of Biological Sciences
Moore 235
Eastern Kentucky University
521 Lancaster Ave.
Richmond, KY 40475-3102
http://www.knps.org

Philateli Lepidopterists of America
Dr. Charles V. Covell, Jr., Secretary, Department of Biology, University of Louisville,
Louisville, KY 40292; 502-588-5942

Society of Kentucky Lepidopterists
Dr. Charles V. Covell, Jr., Secretary, Department of Biology, University of Louisville,
Louisville, KY 40292; 502-588-5942

Louisiana
Louisiana Native Plant Society
216 Caroline Dormon Road
Saline, LA 71070
http://www.lnps.org

Mississippi
The Crosby Arboretum
Mississippi State University Extension
370 Ridge Road
Picayune, MS 39466
http://msstate.edu/dept/crec/camain.html

North Carolina
North Carolina Wildflower Preservation Society
North Carolina Botanical Garden
Totten Garden Center
3375 University of North Carolina
Chapel Hill, NC 27599-3375

The Carolina Butterfly Society
President Dennis Burnette
 4209 Bramlet Place
Greensboro, NC, 27407
Phone 910-299-4342, FAX 910-294-9697

South Carolina
South Carolina Native Plant Society
P.O. Box 759
Pickens, SC 29671
http://www.scnps.org

Southern Appalachian Botanical Society
Newberry College
2100 College Street
Newberry, SC 29108

Southern Lepidopterists' Society
Ronald R. Gatrelle, Chairman and Editor, 126 Wells Road, Goose Creek, SC 29445

Tennessee
Tennessee Native Plant Society
C/O Department of Botany
University of Tennessee
Knoxville, TN 37996-1100

American Association of Field Botanists
P.O. Box 23542
Chattanooga, TN 37422

Wildflower Society
Goldsmith Civic Garden Center
750 Cherry Road
Memphis, TN 38119-4699

NABA-Tennessee Valley
Bill Haley - President
215 McFarland Ave.
Chattanooga, TN 37405
Phone: 800-262-0695 ext. 4056
E-mail: wgh@tnaqua.org
Web site: http://naba.org/chapters/nabatv/

Texas
Native Plant Society of Texas
P.O. Box 3017

Fredericksburg, TX 78624-1929
http://www.npsot.org

Lady Bird Johnson Wildflower Center
4801 La Crosse Avenue
Austin, TX 78739
http://www.wildflower.org

NABA-South Texas
Kim Garwood - President
E-mail: kimgrwd@sbcglobal.net
Web site: http://www.naba.org/chapters/nabast/

NABA-Butterfly Enthusiasts of Southeast Texas (Houston)
Farrar Stockton - President
E-mail: hugahabi@swbell.net
Web site: http://www.naba.org/chapters/nababest/

Tarrant County Butterfly Society
c/o Larry Sweeney
2533 McCart, Fort Worth, TX 76110-2228
Phone 817-923-8474

Dallas County Lepidopterist Society
c/o Dallas Museum of Natural History
P.O. Box 150349, Dallas, TX 75314
Phone 214-421-3466 x232

Virginia
Virginia Native Plant Society
400 Blandy Farm Lane #2
Boyce, VA 22620
http://www.vnps.org

The Butterfly Society of Virginia
Membership Chairman
5333 Challedon Drive
Virginia Beach, VA 23462

West Virginia
West Virginia Native Plant Society
P.O. Box 808
New Haven, WV 25265-0808
http://www.wvnps.org

Appendix III: Butterfly/Moth Attracting Plants by Lighting Conditions

Creating a garden plot in specific lighting conditions such as full sun or full shade requires the gardener to grow plants tolerant of those conditions. If you are wanting to grow a butterfly-enticing plant in specific conditions, these are the profiles found in this book listed by their lighting conditions and in the order they are found in the book.

Full Sun Wildflowers, Flowering Plants, and Vines
Pearly-everlasting (*Anaphalis margaritacea*)
Woman's Tobacco (*Antennaria plantaginifolia*)
Bog Hemp (*Boehmeria cylindrica*)
Spreading Dogbane (*Apocynum androsaemifolium*)
Common Dutchmanspipe (*Aristolochia tomentosa*)
Swamp Milkweed (*Asclepias incarnata*)
Common Milkweed (*Asclepias syriaca*)
Butterflyweed (*Asclepias tuberosa*)
Whorled Milkweed (*Asclepias verticillata*)
Coastal Water-hyssop (*Bacopa monnieri*)
Blue Wild Indigo (*Baptisia australis*)
Horseflyweed (*Baptisia tinctoria*)
Winecup (*Callirhoe involucrata*)
Trumpet Creeper (*Campsis radicans*)
Lambsquarters (*Chenopodium album*)
Partridge Pea (*Chamaecrista fasciculata*)
White Turtlehead (*Chelone glabra*)
Field Thistle (*Cirsium discolor*)
Yellow Thistle (*Cirsium horridulum*)
Swamp Thistle (*Cirsium muticum*)
Rocky Mountain Beeplant (*Cleome serrulata*)
Hogwort (*Croton capitatus*)
Prairie Tea (*Croton monanthogynus*)
Showy Tick Trefoil (*Desmodium canadense*)
Branched Dicliptera (*Dicliptera brachiata*)
Bigleaf Aster (*Eurybia macrophylla*)
Virginia Strawberry (*Fragaria virginiana*)
Thinleaf Sunflower (*Helianthus decapetalus*)
Coral Honeysuckle (*Lonicera sempervirens*)
Sundial Lupine (*Lupinus perennis*)
Common Moonseed (*Menispermum canadense*)
Allegheny Monkeyflower (*Mimulus ringens*)
Virginia Creeper (*Parthenocissus quinquefolia*)
Purple Passionflower (*Passiflora incarnata*)
Hairy Beardtongue (*Penstemon hirsutus*)
Texas Frogfruit (*Phyla nodiflora*)
Blunt-leaf Rabbit-tobacco (*Pseudognaphalium obtusifolium ssp. obtusifolium*)

Black-eyed Susan (*Rudbeckia hirta*)
Sidebeak Pencilflower (*Stylosanthes biflora*)
White Heath Aster (*Symphyotrichum ericoides var. ericoides*)
Smooth Blue Aster (*Symphyotrichum laeve var. laeve*)
Calico Aster (*Symphyotrichum lateriflorum var. lateriflorum*)
Wavyleaf Aster (*Symphyotrichum undulatum*)
Swamp Verbena (*Verbena hastata*)
Narrowleaf Vervain (*Verbena simplex*)
American Wisteria (*Wisteria frutescens*)
Golden Zizia (*Zizia aurea*)

Full Sun Ornamental Grasses
Big Bluestem (*Andropogon gerardii*)
Sideoats Grama (*Bouteloua curtipendula*)
Buffalograss (*Bouteloua dactyloides*)
Saltgrass (*Distichlis spicata*)
Canada Wildrye (*Elymus canadensis*)
Switchgrass (*Panicum virgatum*)
Little Bluestem (*Schizachyrium scoparium*)
Woolgrass (*Scirpus cyperinus*)
Indiangrass (*Sorghastrum nutans*)
Saltmarsh Cordgrass (*Spartina alterniflora*)

Full Sun Native Trees
Pawpaw (*Asimina triloba*)
Common Hackberry (*Celtis occidentalis*)
Cockspur Hawthorn (*Crataegus crus-galli*)
White Ash (*Fraxinus americana*)
Green Ash (*Fraxinus pennsylvanica*)
American Holly (*Ilex opaca*)
Yaupon (*Ilex vomitoria*)
Tuliptree (*Liriodendron tulipifera*)
Red Mulberry (*Morus rubra*)
Virginia Pine (*Pinus virginiana*)
Eastern Cottonwood (*Populus deltoides*)
Wafer Ash (*Ptelea trifoliata*)
Chinkapin Oak (*Quercus muehlenbergii*)
Pin Oak (*Quercus palustris*)
Northern Red Oak (*Quercus rubra*)
Coastal Live Oak (*Quercus virginiana*)
Pussy Willow (*Salix discolor*)
Black Willow (*Salix nigra*)
Sassafras (*Sassafras albidum*)
American Elm (*Ulmus americana*)
Slippery Elm (*Ulmus rubra*)
Hercules' Club (*Zanthoxylum clava-herculis*)

Full Sun Native Shrubs
Indigo Bush (*Amorpha fruticosa*)
Kinnikinnick (*Arctostaphylos uva-ursi*)
Redroot (*Ceanothus herbaceus*)
Beaked Hazelnut (*Corylus cornuta*)
Northern Spicebush (*Lindera benzoin*)
Wax Myrtle (*Morella cerifera*)
Chokecherry (*Prunus virginiana*)
Fragrant Sumac (*Rhus aromatica*)
Winged Sumac (*Rhus copallinum*)
Staghorn Sumac (*Rhus typhina*)
Prairie Willow (*Salix humilis*)
White Meadowsweet (*Spiraea alba*)
Steeplebush (*Spiraea tomentosa*)
Mapleleaf Viburnum (*Viburnum acerifolium*)
Southern Arrowwood (*Viburnum dentatum*)
Hobblebush (*Viburnum lantanoides*)
Prickly Ash (*Zanthoxylum americanum*)

Partial Shade Wildflowers, Flowering Plants, and Vines
Black Cohosh (*Actaea racemosa var. racemosa*)
Pearly-everlasting (*Anaphalis margaritacea*)
Woman's Tobacco (*Antennaria plantaginifolia*)
Bog Hemp (*Boehmeria cylindrica*)
Spreading Dogbane (*Apocynum androsaemifolium*)
Indian Hemp (*Apocynum cannabinum*)
Eastern Red Columbine (*Aquilegia canadensis*)
Common Dutchmanspipe (*Aristolochia tomentosa*)
Swamp Milkweed (*Asclepias incarnata*)
Common Milkweed (*Asclepias syriaca*)
Butterflyweed (*Asclepias tuberosa*)
Whorled Milkweed (*Asclepias verticillata*)
Coastal Water-hyssop (*Bacopa monnieri*)
Winecup (*Callirhoe involucrata*)
Crinkleroot (*Cardamine diphylla*)
Lambsquarters (*Chenopodium album*)
Partridge Pea (*Chamaecrista fasciculata*)
White Turtlehead (*Chelone glabra*)
Swamp Thistle (*Cirsium muticum*)
Rocky Mountain Beeplant (*Cleome serrulata*)
Philadelphia Fleabane (*Erigeron philadelphicus*)
Bigleaf Aster (*Eurybia macrophylla*)
Virginia Strawberry (*Fragaria virginiana*)
American Licorice (*Glycyrrhiza lepidota*)
Thinleaf Sunflower (*Helianthus decapetalus*)

Coral Honeysuckle (*Lonicera sempervirens*)
Sundial Lupine (*Lupinus perennis*)
Common Moonseed (*Menispermum canadense*)
Allegheny Monkeyflower (*Mimulus ringens*)
Virginia Creeper (*Parthenocissus quinquefolia*)
Purple Passionflower (*Passiflora incarnata*)
Yellow Passion Vine (*Passiflora lutea*)
Hairy Beardtongue (*Penstemon hirsutus*)
Texas Frogfruit (*Phyla nodiflora*)
Black-eyed Susan (*Rudbeckia hirta*)
Sidebeak Pencilflower (*Stylosanthes biflora*)
New England Aster (*Symphyotrichum novae-angliae*)
Swamp Verbena (*Verbena hastata*)
Birdfoot Violet (*Viola pedata*)
American Wisteria (*Wisteria frutescens*)
Golden Zizia (*Zizia aurea*)

Partial Shade Ornamental Grasses
Big Bluestem (*Andropogon gerardii*)
Broomsedge Bluestem (*Andropogon virginicus*)
Sideoats Grama (*Bouteloua curtipendula*)
Hairy Grama (*Bouteloua hirsuta*)
Inland Sea Oats (*Chasmanthium latifolium*)
Canada Wildrye (*Elymus canadensis*)
Rice Cut Grass (*Leersia oryzoides*)
Switchgrass (*Panicum virgatum*)
Little Bluestem (*Schizachyrium scoparium*)
Indiangrass (*Sorghastrum nutans*)
Purpletop Tridens (*Tridens flavus*)
Eastern Gamagrass (*Tripsacum dactyloides*)

Partial Shade Native Trees
Pawpaw (*Asimina triloba*)
Cherry Birch (*Betula lenta*)
American Hornbeam (*Carpinus caroliniana*)
Black Hickory (*Carya texana*)
Sugar Hackberry (*Celtis laevigata*)
Common Hackberry (*Celtis occidentalis*)
Flowering Dogwood (*Cornus florida*)
Cockspur Hawthorn (*Crataegus crus-galli*)
Green Hawthorn (*Crataegus viridis*)
American Beech (*Fagus grandifolia*)
White Ash (*Fraxinus americana*)
Green Ash (*Fraxinus pennsylvanica*)
Honey Locust (*Gleditsia triacanthos*)
American Holly (*Ilex opaca*)

Yaupon (*Ilex vomitoria*)
Tuliptree (*Liriodendron tulipifera*)
Red Mulberry (*Morus rubra*)
Redbay (*Persea borbonia*)
Loblolly Pine (*Pinus taeda*)
Eastern Cottonwood (*Populus deltoides*)
Wafer Ash (*Ptelea trifoliata*)
Southern Red Oak (*Quercus falcata*)
Blackjack Oak (*Quercus marilandica*)
Swamp Chestnut Oak (*Quercus michauxii*)
Chinkapin Oak (*Quercus muehlenbergii*)
Pin Oak (*Quercus palustris*)
Willow Oak (*Quercus phellos*)
Northern Red Oak (*Quercus rubra*)
Coastal Live Oak (*Quercus virginiana*)
Black Willow (*Salix nigra*)
Sassafras (*Sassafras albidum*)
Winged Elm (*Ulmus alata*)
American Elm (*Ulmus americana*)
Slippery Elm (*Ulmus rubra*)
Farkleberry (*Vaccinium arboreum*)

Partial Shade Native Shrubs
Indigo Bush (*Amorpha fruticosa*)
Kinnikinnick (*Arctostaphylos uva-ursi*)
New Jersey Tea (*Ceanothus americanus*)
Common Buttonbush (*Cephalanthus occidentalis*)
Sweet Fern (*Comptonia peregrina*)
Redosier Dogwood (*Cornus sericea*)
Beaked Hazelnut (*Corylus cornuta*)
Northern Bush Honeysuckle (*Diervilla lonicera*)
Trailing Arbutus (*Epigaea repens*)
Wild Hydrangea (*Hydrangea arborescens*)
Sheep Laurel (*Kalmia angustifolia*)
Mountain Laurel (*Kalmia latifolia*)
Northern Spicebush (*Lindera benzoin*)
Wax Myrtle (*Morella cerifera*)
Chokecherry (*Prunus virginiana*)
Fragrant Sumac (*Rhus aromatica*)
Staghorn Sumac (*Rhus typhina*)
Saw Palmetto (*Serenoa repens*)
White Meadowsweet (*Spiraea alba*)
Steeplebush (*Spiraea tomentosa*)
Mapleleaf Viburnum (*Viburnum acerifolium*)
Southern Arrowwood (*Viburnum dentatum*)
Hobblebush (*Viburnum lantanoides*)

Full Shade Wildflowers, Flowering Plants, and Vines
Black Cohosh (*Actaea racemosa var. racemosa*)
Bog Hemp (*Boehmeria cylindrica*)
Groundnut (*Apios americana*)
Spreading Dogbane (*Apocynum androsaemifolium*)
Eastern Red Columbine (*Aquilegia canadensis*)
Virginia Snakeroot (*Aristolochia serpentaria*)
Cutleaf Toothwort (*Cardamine concatenata*)
Crinkleroot (*Cardamine diphylla*)
Lambsquarters (*Chenopodium album*)
White Turtlehead (*Chelone glabra*)
Bigleaf Aster (*Eurybia macrophylla*)
American Licorice (*Glycyrrhiza lepidota*)
Thinleaf Sunflower (*Helianthus decapetalus*)
Common Cowparsnip (*Heracleum maximum*)
Common Moonseed (*Menispermum canadense*)
Virginia Creeper (*Parthenocissus quinquefolia*)
Black-eyed Susan (*Rudbeckia hirta*)
Swamp Verbena (*Verbena hastata*)
Birdfoot Violet (*Viola pedata*)
American Wisteria (*Wisteria frutescens*)

Full Shade Ornamental Grasses
Sideoats Grama (*Bouteloua curtipendula*)
Inland Sea Oats (*Chasmanthium latifolium*)
Indiangrass (*Sorghastrum nutans*)

Full Shade Native Trees
Cherry Birch (*Betula lenta*)
American Hornbeam (*Carpinus caroliniana*)
Common Hackberry (*Celtis occidentalis*)
Flowering Dogwood (*Cornus florida*)
Cockspur Hawthorn (*Crataegus crus-galli*)
American Beech (*Fagus grandifolia*)
White Ash (*Fraxinus americana*)
Green Ash (*Fraxinus pennsylvanica*)
American Holly (*Ilex opaca*)
Yaupon (*Ilex vomitoria*)
Tuliptree (*Liriodendron tulipifera*)
Red Mulberry (*Morus rubra*)
Eastern Cottonwood (*Populus deltoides*)
Wafer Ash (*Ptelea trifoliata*)
Pin Oak (*Quercus palustris*)
Black Willow (*Salix nigra*)
Sassafras (*Sassafras albidum*)

Full Shade Native Shrubs

Kinnikinnick (*Arctostaphylos uva-ursi*)
New Jersey Tea (*Ceanothus americanus*)
Common Buttonbush (*Cephalanthus occidentalis*)
Beaked Hazelnut (*Corylus cornuta*)
Northern Bush Honeysuckle (*Diervilla lonicera*)
Trailing Arbutus (*Epigaea repens*)
Northern Spicebush (*Lindera benzoin*)
Chokecherry (*Prunus virginiana*)
Fragrant Sumac (*Rhus aromatica*)
Staghorn Sumac (*Rhus typhina*)
Mapleleaf Viburnum (*Viburnum acerifolium*)
Southern Arrowwood (*Viburnum dentatum*)
Hobblebush (*Viburnum lantanoides*)

www.ingramcontent.com/pod-product-compliance
Lightning Source LLC
Chambersburg PA
CBHW081205280526
45787CB00006B/2327